Great Assistant Principals & the (Great) Principals Who Mentor Them

A Practical Guide

Carole C. Goodman

Christopher S. Berry

EYE ON EDUCATION
6 DEPOT WAY WEST, SUITE 106
LARCHMONT, NY 10538
(914) 833–0551
(914) 833–0761 fax
www.eyeoneducation.com

Library of Congress Cataloging-in-Publication Data

Goodman, Carole C.

  Great assistant principals & the (great) principals who mentor them / Carole C. Goodman, Christopher S. Berry.

     p. cm.

  Great assistant principals and the (great) principals who mentor them

  ISBN 978-1-59667-162-1

  1. Assistant school principals—In-service training. 2. School personnel management. 3. School management and organization. I. Berry, Christopher S. II. Title. III. Title: Great assistant principals and the (great) principals who mentor them.

  LB2831.9.G66 2011

  371.2′012—dc22

                                                                    2010023136

10 9 8 7 6 5 4 3 2 1

Also Available from EYE ON EDUCATION

Get Organized! Time Management for School Leaders
Frank Buck

Solving the Assistant Principal's Puzzle
Douglas L. Hartley

The Principalship from A to Z
Ron Williamson and Barbara R. Blackburn

Classroom Walkthroughs to Improve Teaching and Learning
Donald E. Kachur, Judith A. Stout, and Claudia L. Edwards

**Leading School Change:
9 Strategies to Bring Everybody on Board**
Todd Whitaker

**Rigorous Schools and Classrooms:
Leading the Way**
Ron Williamson and Barbara R. Blackburn

The Principal as Instructional Leader, Second Edition
Sally J. Zepeda

**The Instructional Leader's Guide to
Informal Classroom Observations, Second Edition**
Sally J. Zepeda

**Professional Learning Communities:
An Implementation Guide and Toolkit**
Kathleen A. Foord and Jean M. Haar

Professional Development: What Works
Sally J. Zepeda

Motivating & Inspiring Teachers, Second Edition
Todd Whitaker, Beth Whitaker, and Dale Lumpa

**Data, Data Everywhere: Bringing All the Data
Together for Continuous School Improvement**
Victoria L. Bernhardt

**Creating School Cultures that Embrace Learning:
What Successful Leaders Do**
Tony Thacker, John S. Bell, and Franklin P. Schargel

Meet the Authors

Carole C. Goodman has spent her entire 37-year career in Montgomery County Public Schools in Maryland. She has worked in seven different schools an art teacher, an assistant principal, a middle school principal, and was the founding principal of James Hubert Blake High School, which was truly a labor of love for 13 years. When she moved from the classroom into administration, she never lost her excitement for teaching and transferred that passion into hiring outstanding people and then training and developing them to allow them to reach their maximum potential. She is extremely proud to have mentored and trained 12 assistant principals in her tenure as principal, and currently among their ranks are six principals and one associate superintendent. She has published articles in professional journals on a variety of topics, including student conflict resolution, successful back-to-school nights, and implementing one lunch period in a high school. She has won six major awards: for leadership, in arts and humanities, as an educational leader, and as a humanitarian. She frequently presents to aspiring administrators on implementing change and interview strategies and has presented at local and national conferences on administrative strategies. Carole was recently appointed Associate Superintendent for Human Resources and Development for MCPS, where she is eager to expand her passion for hiring and training outstanding people to an even larger arena.

Christopher Berry has enjoyed a 24-year career as a teacher and administrator for Montgomery County Public Schools in Maryland. For 18 years he taught social studies, most notably Advanced Placement United States History (a subject he still misses teaching), also serving as Department Chair for two high schools. Administratively, he was fortunate to have served as the Signature Program Coordinator in Arts and Humanities, combining his teaching and leadership expertise with his passion for theatre, music, and other art forms. Since 2004 he has worked as an assistant principal, focusing on smaller learning communities for students and empowerment of school-based leadership. In 2007, he was honored as State Assistant Principal of the Year by the Maryland Association of Secondary School Principals. He enjoys presenting at regional and national conferences on leadership models and collaborative systems. Chris was recently appointed principal of James Hubert Blake High School, where he hopes to further the tradition of effective administrative leadership and mentorship.

Contents

Preface

In many ways, the process used to write this book exemplifies the best of a principal–assistant principal relationship. This was a learning experience for both authors, as it needed to be an equal partnership with both bringing much into the process. We quickly discovered what we perhaps already knew, that our styles are very different but our skill sets complement each other perfectly.

Carole's writing style is to jump in feet first and just get something down and then edit away, whereas Chris, always the meticulous planner, used carefully crafted charts and timelines, and labored over each word. Through a back-and-forth process and laughing at ourselves along the way, we hope we produced a valuable resource for both principals and assistant principals.

We are practitioners and worked on this book before basketball games, after the students and staff left for the day, on weekends, before concerts, after dances, etc. The examples we used are based on our own experiences or people we have worked with or know professionally. We have changed some of the facts so that none of our colleagues who believe they see themselves in this book will feel compromised; our intent is to teach through meaningful and real-life examples.

Writing this book was a labor of love because we had the luxury of writing about what we know and think is important. We learned a great deal about ourselves as well as the mentoring relationship between principals and assistant principals and hope you find it helpful.

It is worth noting that when we began to write this book, Carole was principal of James Hubert Blake High School and Chris was assistant principal. By the time final editing had begun, Carole had been appointed associate superintendent for her school district and Chris had replaced her as principal. These real-world events attest to the wisdom and validity of the recommendations in this book and demonstrate that both principal and assistant principal will benefit if they are invested in the processes described in these pages.

Introduction

What This Book Is, What it Isn't, and How to Use It

You have piles of books on educational leadership sitting on your desk and night stand. Why is this one worth your time?

There is no shortage of research, opinions, and helpful advice on the topic of leadership development in education, so we thought it important to delineate what you will find in this book and, perhaps, what you shouldn't be looking for between the covers.

We believe that positive relationships are the basis of a strong educational environment and they require periodic examination. Far too often in the course of a long school day or even longer school year, we administrators do not take the time to stop, consider the big picture, and genuinely reflect on our practice. Sadly, because administrators spend so much of their day reacting, making dozens of split-second decisions and not doing what they had planned on their "To-Do" list, this seems like a luxury. Consider this book our contribution to moving the conversation among administrative teams to something other than the latest disciplinary issue or lunch-duty intrigue.

Making the Case for Strong Relationships

The idea for this book grew out of a series of presentations we made, based on our experiences, at several educational conferences. At the beginning of this process, we noticed that there was a great deal written on the subject of principal and administrative training. What we found less of (in fact, very little at all) was information about the training process for assistant principals. As we constructed our first presentation, we included laundry lists of do's and don'ts to guide assistant principals in their work. Likewise, we included helpful information for principals, because they play a critical and essential role in the development of effective assistant principals. But with each successive presentation, what emerged became the core tenants of this book.

We believe that the principal–assistant principal relationship is perhaps the single most important factor contributing to the quality of the assistant principal leadership development process. Each party in such a relationship brings a perspective that must be respected, understood, and examined as part of this development process. Additionally, although the assistant principal benefits considerably when both parties are fully invested in this process, there is also a tangible developmental payoff for the principal when working with a well-trained assistant principal. Although our goal was to create a guide to selected aspects of developing and maintaining strong assistant principals, ultimately it is equally for both members of the principal–assistant principal partnership.

The education profession is, at its core, a business about relationships. Administrators who are challenged by difficult students sometimes find that, as they attempt to work with difficult parents, "the apple doesn't fall too far from the tree." Assistant principals sometimes find that the most inflexible people they work with are not their students, but the staff members they supervise and interact with on a daily basis. On a larger scale, administrators must navigate the tricky political waters of the district office or work with political leaders so as to marshal support and resources for the programs they think are important. Most of our colleagues would agree that the challenge of becoming an effective assistant principal isn't related to data training, understanding the nuances of student rights, or the technical knowledge required to build a master schedule. Instead, the real challenge is in effectively fostering productive relationships with a myriad of stakeholders. For this reason, we believe that the mentor relationship that both new and veteran assistant principals have with their principal is the cornerstone upon which all other competencies are built.

Roadblocks to Assistant Principal Development: Two Perspectives

It is important to acknowledge two sets of givens related to assistant principal training and development. The first is that the challenge of learning how to be an effective assistant principal is not always within the assistant principal's control. Many educators work in small districts where there may not be many administrative opportunities. If they are fortunate enough to become an assistant principal, it is unlikely that there is a formal training program in place. The assistant principal is often left to fend for herself, which is why there is a great need for a strong mentor principal. But what about the situation where a new assistant principal is committed to a training process, but doesn't have a principal who is invested in the assistant principal's success or professional development?

Sometimes an assistant principal is "pigeon-holed" at the outset of her new position, based on her previous experiences. If a new assistant principal has been a guidance counselor, there may be the assumption that he will be most effective if focuses primarily (if not solely) on student issues, student advocacy, and parent outreach. If the principal assigns duties to the assistant principal based on this premise, there are very few growth opportunities available to the assistant principal. The area the new assistant principal has the least control over is the skill-set he brings (or doesn't bring) to his new position. How does he compensate for knowledge or experience that he just doesn't have?

Many principals find themselves in a less-than-ideal position to be a mentor, often though no fault of their own. For the new principal, it may be that they are "figuring out" their new position and dealing with the big picture issues of running a school, at the same time they should be mentoring their assistant principals. In some situations an assistant principal rises to the principalship in the school where he works and suddenly he is supervising the same professionals who were his peers the day before. Worse yet, one of his colleagues may have also interviewed for the principalship. A new principal may inherit an administrative team that has some weak links. Some principals don't necessarily want or believe they have the time or know how to cultivate talent in others. The roadblock in this instance is a double whammy as it directly affects the effectiveness of the principal, the assistant principal, and, ultimately, the school.

These are not extreme examples. Most administrators can probably see themselves in one or more of these situations. And while in many cases these are instances beyond the control of the individual, this may not be entirely the case. This book does not attempt to be a be-all-end-all solution for difficult situations. It will, however, examine many of these instances and other specific examples and scenarios where the solution lies not just within the individuals in the assistant principal–principal relationship, but more importantly in the work they do together.

What This Book Is and Isn't

We also believe it is important to introduce the practical framework for this book because it is important to understand that "what you see is what you get." This book is not based on years of formalized research, nor is it based on theory.

We offer our own observations, experience, and the experiences of others that have resonated with our colleagues; the ones that result in affirmative nodding heads during the course of a presentation or the "I've been there" look in dialogues. Our intention is to produce an informative read that, at different points, people would recognize their own situation or circumstances and would be anecdotal, practical, and, hopefully, inspire reflection, as well as be thought-provoking. Every example or scenario is based in fact, and either is about people we know, have worked with, or our own experiences.

We both strongly believe that we "stand on the shoulders of giants," namely the people who have been our mentors and administrative role models, as well as our current administrative colleagues who we continue to work alongside every day in our school. We both feel fortunate to have many of the positive ideas we outline in this work modeled for us on a daily basis. It's important to note that we have taken the liberty to alter certain circumstances, genders, and curricular areas within some of our examples to maintain confidentiality and discretion.

Other Than as a Doorstop, How Can You Use this Book?

The chapters are grouped sequentially in a relative progression but each one is also designed to stand alone. The content can be understood in any order depending on your interest and inclination. Each chapter provides practical examples for the assistant principal, the principal, or both together. Although the reader could certainly digest most of the text in one sitting, we think it would be beneficial to read one or two related chapters at a time and consider the following questions as they apply:

♦ What have I read that applies to my professional situation or resonates with me personally?

♦ What doesn't apply or isn't valid in my district, school, or circumstances?

♦ What are the one or two ideas worth exploring or reflecting upon with others?

♦ If something is worth exploring or implementing, what are my next steps?

We hope this book functions as a means of having both new and veteran assistant principals and mentor principals read and reflect on the questions above, or wherever the conversation leads them. Our goal is to increase the communication between principals and assistant principals and enhance school leadership on all levels, for the ultimate benefit of the students whom we serve.

The Traditional Assistant Principal in Nontraditional Times

The changing role of the assistant principal requires rethinking what's important in their development.

Once Upon a Time

In the not so recent past, the assistant principal played a clearly defined role in the life of a school. They were first and foremost disciplinarians, handling student issues that were too serious for the classroom teacher, but did not require the attention of the principal. Second, they were managers of much of the organizational structure of the school—bell schedules, lunch duty, chaperone duty, textbook and material management, and a host of "other duties as assigned." Finally, they served as the conduit of the principal, in charge of the implementation of decisions from the principal and district leadership, the loyal lieutenant in a top-down chain of command. Often, the assistant principal was cast as the villain, determined to make students' lives miserable and confound both teachers and parents alike. But for today's assistant principal, nothing could be further from the truth.

Like many large institutions, schools in the immediate post-World War II era bear little resemblance to those of today. As the requirements have changed for school systems to meet the needs of a growing and more complex student population, so have the roles and demands of school leaders.

Principals provide instructional leadership in the form of vision and accountability, and department chairs/team leaders provide leadership on subject content. More recently, some new leadership roles have evolved within many secondary schools across the country, including staff development specialists, content area coordinators, literacy coaches, business operations managers and data analysis specialists. The dynamics related to these new and evolutionary roles has also changed, and the principal is less likely to rule with an autocratic, unquestioned leadership style. In short, there is more give and take of all issues of leadership, and decisions which were previously made with little input from other stakeholders have become (or must become) consensus oriented.

Assistant Principal 2.0: The Evolution From Training to Leadership Development

As a result, in today's educational environment assistant principals, by design and necessity, are called upon to do more big picture and management tasks, in addition to delegating many school-based initiatives to others. They coordinate the efforts of those in emerging leadership roles while still attending to the day-to-day business of supervising teachers and, first and most importantly, working with students in a wide variety of ways. What is the difference between the traditional role and the new requirements of leadership for today's assistant principals? How should principals mentor assistant principals to prepare them to take on this new role in the evolving world of education? And perhaps most importantly, how can administrative teams, under a principal's guidance, structure their duties and responsibilities in a way that not only benefits the school, but allows them to grow as professionals?

Today's assistant principals must be critically important members of the school's administrative leadership team. As second-in-command to the principal, they must be well-versed and prepared for numerous aspects of school leadership. They must be properly trained and highly capable of taking a leadership role in the instructional program, and comfortable working closely with very different constituency groups, students, staff, parents, the greater community, and central office personal. In addition, they must have skills and competencies in a wide variety of areas, including management strategies, data analysis, hiring practices, human relations interactions, and school finances, and have an understanding of the politics, both nationally and locally, that impact schools. They need to know how to secure a multitude of resources and to cultivate relationships that will benefit the school. They must develop outstanding communications skills, both oral and written, and they also must be willing and prepared to make important decisions. This is a huge shift from the days when assistant principals spent the majority of their time dealing with students who cut class and assigning them detention.

Just as the role of the assistant principal has evolved, so must the leadership development associated with the position. Traditionally, assistant principal training, when it even occurred, was "one size fits all," done sporadically and often in isolation. At worst, in too many school districts, a comprehensive training plan doesn't exist at all, and assistant principals are left to experience the all-too-familiar "trial by fire." This plan (or lack of one) is based on a simple cornerstone: the principal tells the assistant principal what to do and the assistant principal does it. For resources, the assistant principal is often dependent upon artifacts to decipher from the previous assistant principal, in the form of dusty three-ring binders on their bookshelf. Most of the time, assistant principals in this situation are put in the position of "depending on the kindness of strangers," namely rapid-fire advice from their new colleagues, prefaced with the phrase, "This is how we do it here." Formal training, if it exists at all, might come via degree or certificate programs, or "drive-through" training in which the assistant principal is declared the expert after a three-hour directive session. If there is the rare opportunity to attend a professional conference, the chance to do meaningful followup or training with other colleagues is rarer still. In short, this is not the best way to cultivate leadership talent in education.

The missing ingredient in the leadership-training recipe is the relationship that the assistant principal and principal develop in this process. How well an assistant principal is trained and how the principal sees her role and responsibility in mentoring can make a tremendous difference in the career path of the assistant principal and, ultimately, the overall effectiveness of the school. People become assistant principals for many reasons and bring a wide range of experiences, skills and abilities to the position. It is incumbent upon the principal to evaluate where each assistant principal is professionally and what training is needed to help her be most effective, whether she is a brand new novice assistant principal, fresh out of the classroom, or one with 25 years of experience who needs to refresh and retool her skills to meet changing demands.

The Assistant Principal Assignment: Old School vs. New School of Thought

When a principal has multiple assistant principals under his direction, traditionally the easiest thing to do is to look at the skill-set of each individual and assign roles commensurate with their individual strengths as they align with the needs of the school. In many ways, it makes sense to have the former football coach serve as the disciplinarian as he has a presence, is highly respected, and does not put up with any nonsense from students. The assistant principal who was a math teacher is usually assigned the responsibilities of building the master schedule and organizing all testing, the school calendar, and any other detail-oriented tasks. And the assistant principal who was a highly effective chair of the English department and is seen as the instructional leader, is the one who is assigned to manage curriculum issues and observe and evaluate teachers. Principals may assess the "soft skills" of assistant principals and then assign tasks accordingly. For the school where there is only one assistant principal, they are expected to assume all of the administrative tasks the principal does not do, which can be overwhelming.

For many, many years, this is how the majority of high schools were organized and it is still common practice. Doesn't it make sense to assign assistant principals tasks and roles they are most comfortable performing and best suited for? Doesn't this assure a more efficiently and effectively run school? Why wouldn't a principal choose to position people where they are comfortable and are certain they will be effective as school leaders? This certainly may arguably be the most expedient and efficient way to assign responsibilities. It may also ensure that the assistant principals are comfortable and familiar with their job responsibilities. The school may even run effectively. But the downside is evident in too many administrative teams: stagnation of assistant principals in their position, single-dimensional leadership, and a lack of professional growth.

Then there are other principals who use another transition plan. When one assistant principal leaves, and a new assistant principal is hired, the new assistant principal is expected to plug into where the previous person left off. If the master scheduler retires, the newly hired assistant principal is assigned that task, sometimes even when it is not a good match for her abilities and she has other strengths and skills that might be beneficial elsewhere in the administrative organization. There may even be another assistant principal who has the experience needed to take on that responsibility, yet this change of assignment is not considered. The new assistant principal is given the task of creating the master schedule even though a responsibility this great is probably not the first major assignment she should take on, as she probably does not have the ability or experience to tackle it effectively. The same goes for the remaining responsibilities that the previous assistant principal had. The new assistant principal picks up as best she can with these duties, regardless of her experience, and learns a great deal on the job. But who would allow this situation to unfold in the first place? The two most likely suspects are a principal who sees this choice as expedient and doesn't want to rock the boat with the other members of his administrative team, and the rest of the administrative team who are comfortable with their current duties and don't believe that a change in their responsibilities is necessary because someone else left.

A third option is to take a fresh approach and realize that anytime someone leaves and there is a new addition to an administrative team, they bring something to the table and the team dynamics change. This may be an excellent opportunity and a good time to shift gears and shake some things up, allowing for new experiences and a fresh perspective for everyone.

A New Approach to the Assistant Principal Assignment: Shuffle and Deal

In one school, an administrative "deck of cards" model has become the norm for determining what assistant principal assignments will be each year, even the years when no one leaves and the team remains constant. The principal has a clear vision that an essential component of her role is to provide training and professional development to the assistant principals, and strategically rotating assigned responsibilities is one way to ensure this mentoring occurs.

Each summer, on a day when the students and staff are nowhere to be found, this administrative team sits around a table with a list of every task, initiative, and responsibility that needs to be assigned and accomplished in the coming year. This includes supervision of departments, grade-level responsibilities, large management tasks such as the master schedule, master calendar, testing, and community liaisons to groups such as the Parent Teacher Association (PTA), athletic boosters, special education parents, NAACP, and Latino parent groups. Some major responsibilities clearly must be taken on by the principal, but many others need to be divided up among the administrative team. In this school, tasks are determined to fall under four categories: Leadership, Supervision and Evaluation, Management, and Committee/Group Liaison. The team goes so far as to produce a chart that is a continual work in progress as this process unfolds.

Then the conversation begins: An extensive and collegial dialogue that demonstrates how division of responsibilities can best serve the school but also help each assistant principal grow and develop their personal professional skill-set. Each assistant principal thinks aloud about what responsibilities they want to retain from the previous year and why they want to keep them. The conversation moves on to what new challenges each assistant principal is interested in taking on, and what they potentially want to pass along to someone else, if reasonable. There is back and forth, scribbling and crossing out, "horse trading" of responsibilities. There are a lot of hypothetical questions posed: "What ifs…" and "What would be the advantage of…?" and "What's the growth opportunity for me if…?" The ultimate product is a clear chart of each assistant principal's professional assignments, which is crystal clear to all school stakeholders.

For this team, the discussion is simultaneously focused on what is in the best interests of the school and students, but also whose turn it is for a particular challenge. Departmental supervision usually presents this type of opportunity. One year in the same "deck of cards" school, the science department had new leadership and one assistant principal really wanted to continue to supervise that department. He felt he had developed a positive rapport with the new department chair and the entire department was showing significant growth and moving in a positive direction. He very much wanted to continue working with them. On the other hand, the newest assistant principal was in the district's training and development program and one requirement was supervision of either the math or English department as they were aligned to state testing. The social studies department was going to have a large number of teachers up for evaluation in the coming year so it made sense for the assistant principal who supervised that department to have a lighter load elsewhere as they would have many observations and evaluations to write up. There was also an ineffective teacher who was going to require a significant amount of supervision and attention to either show improvement or documentation would need to be gathered to recommend him for dismissal. Whichever assistant principal worked with that teacher would need to devote a great deal of time to that process.

The principal had some specific ideas about who should take on which specific responsibilities but was also open to hearing the assistant principals' preferences and rationale. Since this process is adhered to year after year and the expectations are clear to the assistant principals, the discussion was very collegial and productive, and in many cases was about making sure they were not overloading any one person. The discussion was not about power struggles or anyone trying to shirk responsibilities. An added benefit was that because everyone had a say in the conversation, there wasn't any bickering or complaining and everyone ultimately ended up satisfied with their assignment. The administrative team left the table with a clear understanding of how and why responsibilities were divided up for the coming year, what supports they could expect and why this not only benefitted the school, but was in everyone's best professional interests. It is an annual best practice that works extremely well at that school.

Trying New Things

Clearly not all administrative teams function as effectively as this one does. Most teams have varying degrees of professional and personal trust that may or may not allow for this level of collegiality and give and take. Every new administrative team begins with small exercises in learning how to work together, progressing to greater levels of cooperation, true collaboration and ultimately, trust. The core relationship, however, is that between the assistant principal and the principal mentor. In addition, the role of the assistant principal and challenges they face must be examined. Although there continues to be a strong need for traditional formalized training for assistant principals, the informal, ongoing training that comes through principal mentoring is the heart of school-based leadership development.

In the school with one assistant principal, this may be a bigger challenge as her role is larger and the principal must depend on her to do more. Although there may be fewer students to supervise, the management tasks remain the same, regardless of the size of the school. The assistant principal and principal may not have the luxury of rotating certain responsibilities, but it is important that the assistant principal still have opportunities to grow and develop professionally.

The bottom line is this: Today's high stakes educational environment demands effective administrative leadership. The traditional cookie-cutter approach to training an assistant principal is less and less valid or effective. Principals and assistant principals need to keep an open mind and be willing to try new things and wide-ranging professional development and opportunities for assistant principals, which ultimately transfer into better-run, more innovative schools, and result in greater student achievement. Effective principals grow leaders within their schools. And among the ranks of their assistant principals may lie future principals and even superintendents, when they are provided with well-developed and thought-out experiences, mentoring, guidance, encouragement, and opportunities.

2

The Difference Between Principal's Job and the Assistant Principal's Job

Although most people perceive assistant principals to be "junior" principals, there are fundamental differences in the role and relationship of both positions.

The Deceiving Look of the "Glamorous Principalship"

Many assistant principals see themselves as the person who actually runs the school and often wonder exactly what the principal does all day. From the assistant principal's perspective, the principal spends much of his time out of the building at endless meetings, on the phone, buried under piles of paperwork, and in conferences in his office with the door closed. Meanwhile the assistant principal is left to do the heavy lifting and has the day-to-day interactions with students, parents and teachers and manages the instructional leadership of the school. The assistant principal is on the front lines with hall duty, cafeteria duty, bus duty, coordinating endless activities, mediating disagreements, dealing with often trivial student issues, sitting through parent/teacher meetings, calling irate parents, intercepting interlopers, etc. For some assistant principals, it feels like (metaphorically) they spend their days wiping noses and applying band-aids. The principal's job looks interesting and glamorous whereas the assistant principal's job resembles grunt work. Because the assistant principal views the principal's job as exciting, appealing, and easy, doesn't mean that it actually is. So what are the real differences? Why does the principal get the big bucks?

Much like the chairman of the board and the CEO of a corporation, the principal establishes the "big picture," working with numerous stakeholder groups, while the assistant principal carries out the day-to-day operations of the organization. The assistant principal (CEO) may know the finer details of situation and make numerous decisions, but in all cases they should be guided by ideas that promote the vision of the principal (the chairman). Even the most open-minded of principals who does her best to keep her assistant principals apprised of all situations may not share some of the responsibilities she shoulders that are difficult to quantify. Part of the reality is the old adage "the buck stops here," as everything in the school is ultimately the responsibility of the principal. Parents, rightly or wrongly, will often start at the top to resolve issues. And anything a principal delegates to anyone—

anything at all—whether it does or doesn't go well, ultimately comes back to the principal.

One big difference between the role of the principal and that of the assistant principal is dealing with politics. Whether it is navigating a community issue, hand-holding litigious parents, lobbying school board members, or interacting with central office personnel, effective principals are skilled politicians. They must walk the fine line of lobbying for the needs of their school, without stepping on toes. They are often called to make presentations at the district level to a variety of stakeholders and must be well-versed in all aspects of their school as well as the larger context and educational landscape. They are often pitted against colleagues at other district schools as scores are compared and analyzed. Principals must be skilled in dealing with the media as a poorly worded quote to a reporter can be a career ender. Although assistant principals may get a taste of these experiences, ultimately these are the times when the principal is on the front lines, not the assistant principal.

The Rhyme and Reason of Delegation

Principals have numerous responsibilities and there are many reasons they may delegate some of them to their assistant principal. Sometimes it's because the assistant principal has a better grasp of a particular situation and is truly the best person to deal with it. Or assistant principal has a solid relationship with the parties involved and will be highly effective in solving the problem at hand. In other cases, the principal is working to train the assistant principal to handle certain types of issues as part of the assistant principal's professional growth and development and delegating is in the assistant principal's best interests.

An example of this was when a principal delegated the development of the school safety and security plan to an assistant principal. The assistant principal dove in, secure in the knowledge that he had covered all bases and could easily produce an effective, detailed, and comprehensive document. But when the principal reviewed the plan with the assistant principal, he pointed out some of the many nuances the assistant principal missed, such as who would be responsible for the wheelchair-bound students, who was to be the point of contact should the entire school be evacuated to the local church, and who was to be responsible for gathering and securing all of the student emergency information. The principal was not trying to embarrass or undermine the assistant principal, but rather was working to teach him to view all facets of something as seemingly simple and straight forward, but actually quite intricate and complex, as the safety and security emergency plan. The principal's agenda in this case was to ensure that the assistant principal was familiar and comfortable with all aspects of the security plan in the event he was in charge when there was a crisis situation.

The principal might delegate representation at a meeting to the assistant principal, perhaps based on their gender, race, or some other factor that would be perceived as positive by the other attendees at the meeting and might help move the situation. Or the task might just be something the principal really does not have time to do or want to do for some reason, legitimate or not, and the principal pulls rank. Effective principals do not ask their assistant principals to do anything they would not do or haven't done themselves, but there are many times when it is appropriate for the principal to delegate. Often this is a result of the magnitude of appointments and events a principal must attend on any given day. In some situations, having the assistant principal handle a sticky situation leaves another level of appeal at the school, should the issue not be resolved by the assistant principal. In many cases, this actually sends a positive message to parents that the principal has confidence in the assistant principal's ability to deal with the issue at hand in an appropriate manner.

The (Temporary) View from the Big Chair

The big picture differences between the role of the principal and the role of the assistant principal can be the most difficult for the assistant principal to grasp. Most assistant principals have some experience being in charge when the principal is out of the building, sometimes for a day, but sometimes for an extended period of time. Depending on the length of time the assistant principal is in charge, it can be a very real and extremely valuable experience or it can be frustrating without a meaningful learning outcome. Short-term decisions can be a learning experience for the assistant principal, but when parents and staff know the principal is returning, the assistant principal's decisions may be regarded as a temporary inconvenience until the principal returns. In many cases, people will simply wait for the principal to return and then appeal to the principal if they did not agree with the assistant principal's decision. If the principal has ensured that the assistant principal is well prepared, he should stand behind the assistant principal's decision, reinforcing the assistant principal's autonomy and demonstrating significant support on the part of the principal.

Before any assistant principal is left in charge, an effective principal ensures that the assistant principal has undergone considerable training, that there has been extensive communication between the principal and the assistant principal, and that the assistant principal is confident and prepared to handle the challenge. In addition, it is incumbent on the principal to let the staff know that the assistant principal is acting principal in her absence and that the principal has complete confidence in any decision the assistant principal makes and will support those decisions.

The assistant principal in-charge, in turn, needs to trust her good judgment, but not lose sight of what the principal would want as an outcome in decisions. At times there is a difference in philosophy between what the assistant principal believes should happen and what they know they principal would do. In the end, the assistant principal needs to come back once again to the adage, "the buck stops here." If there is fallout from the situation, ultimately it will land on the principal's desk. It's better for the assistant principal to "channel the thoughts of the principal" than make a choice that the principal will have difficulty supporting. One way to ensure this happens is for the assistant principal to use the human resources around him to bounce ideas off of to make sure his decisions are sound. Some of the worst decisions made by an assistant principal who is acting principal are made as a power play without vetting them through other members of the administrative team.

In one situation, a principal was out on a medical leave for a three-week period, and the senior, veteran assistant principal was acting principal. During this period, in addition to the day-to-day responsibilities, there was a huge blowup with a parent who was upset and extremely unhappy with the basketball coach over his son's playing time, alleging racism on both the part of the coach and the assistant principal. The athletic director tried to appease the parent, but the parent was unreasonable, threatening, and belligerent. The assistant principal did his best, but ultimately the situation took on a life of its own and resulted in a parent protest that went to the district level. The assistant principal personalized what happened and was so demoralized that he basically shut down for the remainder of the year and ultimately left for another school. The difficulty for the assistant principal in this situation was not having the principal there to back him up in his decisions and intervene when the situation got ugly and overwhelming. He didn't use or wasn't able to access other supports, so he felt isolated and eventually paralyzed when the situation got out of hand. This was a highly skilled assistant principal and the situation was most unfortunate.

Shining a Spotlight on the Assistant Principal

If the assistant principal shoulders responsibility when things go wrong, it's equally important for the principal to give credit where it is due when things go well. Effective assistant principals understand that when they are charged with implementing the details of projects, it is on behalf of the principal. When these tasks go right, the principal as the "visionary" or chairman is often given the accolades, even when he may have had little to do with the real implementation. But when a principal is consistent about publically recognizing who really did the work, there are many tangible benefits, among them the assistant principal feels valued for her work, the sense of loyalty and trust between the assistant principal and principal is enhanced, and the principal demonstrates a sense of selflessness. Giving credit for good work is an affirmation that there is a distinct difference between the job of the assistant principal and the job of principal, and that both are important.

One assistant principal was charged with implementing a plan for phasing in a new program for English language learners. The community was a very homogenous one and there was great trepidation as to how this program would change the school. There was concern that the students would be intolerant and staff were very nervous about how to interact with students with limited English proficiency. The assistant principal developed a plan that was rolled out over the course of a school year. Staff heard from a panel of nonnative English-speaking students about their experiences at another school and what would help them be successful students in their new school. A community liaison spoke to the faculty about resource supports she was able to provide for students. A professional development day was spent watching a film about a family's journey from Guatemala to the United States and the hardships they underwent to arrive in the United States. The assistant principal arranged for the film to be shown in the school auditorium and even provided popcorn. She also arranged for a question-and-answer period following the film, and later screened the film for student leaders to help increase their understanding and knowledge of cultural differences.

When the next school year began and the new students arrived, their transition went extremely smoothly and they were welcomed with open arms by the school community. The principal was elated and went so far as to share the assistant principal's plan, giving her the full credit, with district leadership and encouraging the use of this plan by other schools opening English as Second Language programs. The assistant principal felt extremely validated for all of her hard work and was very appreciative of the principal's accolades.

The View from the Top Through the Principal's Looking Glass

The stark reality is that as close as principals may feel to their assistant principals or other staff members, they are still regarded as "the boss" and there will always be a divide. The job of the principal can be a lonely one as it is far more common for school staff, assistant principals included, who are heading out to lunch on a professional day or in the summer to say, "Can we bring you anything?" rather than "Would you like to join us?" For principals who have risen through the ranks of a school, or those who believe they have collegial relationships with their staff, this can be particularly painful. One principal, who enjoyed entertaining, hosted an annual summer barbecue for her leadership team and also hosted the annual staff holiday party until staff told her it was perceived as an obligation and people did not want to go. She stopped the practice and took a step back when she realized that her hospitality was never reciprocated and probably not appreciated. This was less about people "liking" her and more about position power, but nonetheless was a hurtful reminder about how lonely it can be at the top.

At the end of the day, it is the principal who shoulders every burden in the school; it is the principal who is considered the face of and spokesperson for the school. The principal stresses over central office demands; trash in the parking lot; a drop in test scores; the ramifications of a fight in the community; PTA issues; finding a long-term substitute for a teacher going on sick leave; telling a staff member that their position has been cut for next year; lobbying for a traffic light; evaluating an ineffective teacher; dealing with the media when something bad happens; and the multitude of issues and politics involving students, staff, and parents. This is not to say that the principal works harder or more diligently than his assistant principals. The work of an assistant principal often has more of a beginning, middle, and end on a daily and yearly basis. The principal's work is ongoing and, seemingly, never done. The assistant principal has a greater ability to focus on one task or aspect of leadership, while the principal, by design, not only has to wear multiple hats, but completely different outfits on a given day. It is less important to weigh the ways in which one position is more difficult that the other, it is probably more significant to grasp that these two roles are more "different" than most people (even educators) understand.

Every single thing that happens in a school, regardless of its relative importance, is ultimately the responsibility of the principal. This intangible factor, and not the day-to-day running of the school, is the main difference between the job of the assistant principal and that of the principal. The reality is that this one distinction is perhaps the most difficult for even the best-trained and most talented assistant principal to comprehend. In the end, it is not critical for the assistant principal to completely understand the principal's job. But time after time, several weeks into their first principalship, a former assistant principal will call their former principal and declare, "I finally get it; I understand what you really did all day. You made it look so easy."

3

The Assistant Principal Role: What the Students Need

From knowing their name to meeting their needs as young adults, effectively managing student relationships requires skill and commitment.

School-based educators need to always remember that our number one purpose is to educate, work with, support, and develop the students we serve in the school community. An assistant principal wears many hats and takes on many roles and responsibilities, but needs to recognize that it is critical to keep students' needs in the forefront of every decision.

"Getting to Know You…"

Secondary schools can be organized in many different ways and assistant principal assignments usually, but not always, include supervision of students. However, if student supervision and discipline is part of an assistant principal's assignment, they are usually assigned by grade level or alphabetically, and the very best thing an assistant principal can do is get to know the students in their caseload in a positive way and as quickly as possible.

There are many strategies assistant principals can use to get to know students. It cannot be overstated how important it is to be visible and approachable in and around the school. As one assistant principal remarked, "I can get a lot of the same work accomplished sitting at my desk firing off e-mails. But unless I'm out meeting students and interacting with them, I don't really know what's going on." The easiest, most obvious, and often most effective way is to say a simple "good morning" to students in the hallways on a regular basis. Students almost always respond in a positive manner to a friendly greeting; in fact, most everyone does. Remarking to students that you saw them earlier in the day mastering a science lab, scoring a goal in the field hockey game last night, or asking about an older sibling who graduated from the school serves to build common ground. Most students will never admit this, but they like to be recognized and acknowledged.

Another important strategy that cannot be overemphasized is to learn individual students' names. This can be a challenge in a large school but this is incredibly powerful, especially when a student has no idea the assistant principal even knows who they are, and it can completely disarm them in a positive way. Just the fact that someone bothered to learn the student's name speaks volumes, especially if it is for a positive or benign reason. Conversely, when the assistant principal knows a student's name, it can signal the beginning of a relationship. Some districts have student pictures available online, which is extremely helpful to the administrators as it reinforces their ability to learn names. If this is not the case, a yearbook can be an excellent aid in learning student names.

One assistant principal who is traditionally the administrator for the ninth grade in his high school makes it a habit to get the yearbooks from both middle schools that feed his school at the end of each school year. He uses this as a tool to familiarize himself with the students he will be working with the next year. Establishing positive connections with students always makes the job of the assistant principal easier, and learning names makes students feel valued and recognized, particularly when it is not a student who is on everyone's radar. There is nothing more powerful than a student being greeted by name on the first day of school by the assistant principal who has learned names and faces before he even meets the students.

Keeping It Positive, Keeps It Productive

Another benefit to knowing student names and the informal interaction of the hallway and classroom is that the first interaction with the administrator can be a good one. For potentially problematic students, if the first contact the student has with the assistant principal is a positive one, it makes future conflicts easier to work through. It also gives the assistant principal a frame of reference about the student which may be neutral or positive rather than always beginning with negatives in discipline situations. One assistant principal said, "Some days when I'm in my office, I feel like all of my interactions with students are about bad things. Getting out and talking to kids gives me the opportunity to prove that isn't so."

Positive relationships can go a long way when something happens and the assistant principal needs to rely on students to provide information or assistance. A student is far more likely to come forward and talk about a situation to an assistant principal when the student believes he knows and respects her. The best compliment an assistant principal can get from students, is to be told she is considered fair. Although fair isn't always equal, students need to believe that if they have a problem or an issue, they will be listened to and treated fairly. There are simple ways to accomplish this. Many assistant principals make it a point to come out from behind their desk and sit next to a student or at a table in an empathetic fashion when the situation warrants. Another administrator makes it a point to listen to everything the student has to say before he begins to speak. This allows the student to get everything out, even when they are angry and often gives the assistant principal far more information about the situation. Yet another makes a habit of telling the student everything they plan to say to the student's parent before making the phone call, in the name of transparency with the student. It doesn't change the job the assistant principal has to do, but many of today's youth equate fairness with basic respect. For one assistant principal, validation of the job he was doing came this way: When a student who committed a serious crime, was escorted out of school in handcuffs by a police officer, and called out to the assistant principal, "I want you to know that I respect you and know you were doing your job," despite all that happened, the student recognized that he was treated fairly by the assistant principal.

Knowing Their Name Isn't Enough: Knowing What They Need

As the role of the assistant principal has evolved, examining and understanding student data has become a critically important aspect of the job. The traditional disciplinarian has been replaced by the assistant principal who manages all aspects of the students' school life; in fact, they often become the default parent for the time the students spend in school. Assistant principals need to be familiar with student data and have the capacity to develop action plans for educational and behavioral programs for individual students and to work in close concert with school guidance counselors. They need to be familiar with student transcripts and have a thorough understanding of their students' progress toward graduation. This can be complicated when schools have various data management systems and knowledge of a variety of different data programs is necessary. For this reason, it becomes incumbent upon assistant principals to spend time broadening their skill set of seemingly impersonal data programs so as to have a more personal understanding of their students.

Assistant principals who really know their students can have an important influence in getting them to take rigorous classes, or in some cases, run interference if teachers are discouraging them. Assistant principals can initiate the conversation with students about their academic progress and need to remember to check their grades, status of standardized testing and make sure students aren't falling through the cracks. In one situation, a principal met with a graduating senior who needed a recommendation letter for a highly competitive scholarship opportunity. The principal met with the student so as to get to know her better before writing the letter. The principal looked at the student's transcript and was shocked by it. The student began high school in all average level classes with grades of Bs and Cs. By the second semester she was moved to all honors classes and had straight As for the remainder of her high school career. The student was African American and very quiet and clearly had been underestimated and unchallenged in her first semester of high school. She indicated that her assistant principal changed the level of her classes at the end of the first semester at the urging of one of her teachers and the rest was history. Although not every student would necessarily experience that level of success, the fact that the assistant principal and teacher saw a spark in this student, clearly changed her life.

Effective assistant principals look at the whole student and base instructional decisions on what is in the best interests of students. One principal consistently modeled an important instructional strategy for her assistant principals, which turned even a suspension appeal meeting into a problem-solving conference that examined the students' academic progress and needs. This principal had a practice of never sitting down for a meeting with a parent and student without a transcript, report card, attendance history, current grade reports, standardized test data, or any piece of information that helped piece together an accurate picture of the total student. Even if the purpose of the meeting was initially a negative one, perhaps to discuss a disciplinary infraction, the principal was always able to turn the meeting into a productive discussion where the student's academic progress became the most important topic of discussion. In the majority of cases, even the angriest parent left pleased by the shift in the discussion and the outcome of the meeting. In some cases, the student's schedule was changed to include honors or more rigorous classes and a plan was discussed for how the student could be more academically successful. Most parents and students view this kind of interaction as highly positive and respectful of the student as an individual and as a learner.

When moving from an individual student to the larger school context, it becomes challenging for instructional decisions to be made first and foremost about the needs of the students. When an assistant principal is the master scheduler, it is easy to get caught up in which coach wants the last period of the day off, which teachers hate to teach first period, who wants common planning time with another teacher and giving the top teachers all of the choice classes. The reality is, the master schedule must be built and designed in the best interests of the students. Every student deserves the opportunity to have outstanding teachers; the wealth of teacher talents needs to be spread around so the most outstanding teachers do not just teach the most advanced classes. Conversely, the rookie teachers should not get the lowest level or most difficult classes. There is a tendency to give novice teachers the lowest levels and often most challenging classes to teach, which is not fair to either the teacher or their students. As an instructional leader, there are often many political reasons for instructional decisions but the needs of the students, particularly the neediest students, should come before teacher preferences in the schedule.

When What the Student Needs Has Little to Do with the Classroom

In some cases, the assistant principal must deal with difficult sociological-emotional issues with students. When assistant principals have positive relationships with their students, students will often confide in them, sometimes about difficult personal issues. One assistant principal had a teacher report that a female student cut a class. When she called the student in and confronted her about it, the student burst into tears and said she actually cut the class so she would get caught and sent to the assistant principal. She told the assistant principal she had been at a party on the weekend and drank so much that she was certain she had unprotected sex with possibly multiple partners and was terrified she was pregnant. The assistant principal was able to work with the student, walk her over to the school nurse (who in this case worked for the public health department so could discuss options with the student) and convinced her to confide in her parents. These steps led to the student getting help with her alcohol and peer issues as well as counseling about sexual activity. The assistant principal played a key role in helping the student get the assistance and support she needed.

One of the factors that allow effective assistant principals to play this role is their understanding of how to connect students to other resources, many outside the school building. In today's educational landscape, it's important to be familiar with social service networks, police assistance programs, drug and alcohol programs, and in some cases, child protective services. One assistant principal said the school-based social worker in his school was always his "go to" person: "If I don't have an answer, I know she does." Many such professionals in and out of schools support these efforts. School counselors, psychologists, healthcare professionals, social workers, and child advocates can help the assistant principal navigate difficult student situations requiring outside intervention.

In another case, a male assistant principal was surprised when a bright but very disruptive female student told him she was pregnant and had an appointment scheduled at an abortion clinic. She came from tragic family circumstances with a drug-addicted mother and had dreams of attending college. The assistant principal became a tremendous support system for the student through her remaining years of high school and worked with her guidance counselor to help her get college scholarships. He kept the student's situation confidential and periodically checked up on her. The hug (through tears) she gave him at graduation meant so much more than anyone observing could have imagined and she kept in touch with him through her college years.

The assistant principal who sees his role as developing and working with the total child on academic and sociological-emotional issues in addition to discipline, reaps the rewards that often comes much later in the process of dealing with students. And often the rewards are the greatest from the most challenging and difficult students. They are the ones who followup years later to let the assistant principal know they made a significant difference to them, that they turned out okay, and to say thank you.

4

The Assistant Principal Role: What the Staff Needs

Allies or adversaries? A look at the staff–assistant principal relationship through several lenses.

Recognizing the Difference Between
What Teachers Want and Need

Most administrators rise from the ranks of the classroom teacher, and assume when they become an assistant principal, that they will understand the needs of their staff colleagues most completely. Most assistant principals remember what qualities they admired in assistant principals they worked with, and, more importantly, what they wanted and needed from them to forge a strong working relationship. One assistant principal summarized what she quickly learned about the staff and their relationship with the assistant principal: "What they want is for you to make the trains run on time. What they really need is validation, guidance, and being held accountable for their stake in your school."

"Making the trains run on time" is shorthand for making the routine management decisions that allows a school to progress effectively on a day-to-day basis. Teachers want special bell schedules well in advance, so that they can adjust their instruction and plan appropriately. If a teacher sends a student to the office with a discipline referral, they want to know that action was taken and suitable consequences were assigned. If the computer network is not functioning, the staff wants the assistant principal in charge of technology to make the phone calls, restore the network quickly, and give regular updates about progress toward fixing the problem. These are seemingly simple things, but in the teaching world, they mean everything. As one rookie assistant principal reflected, tongue firmly in cheek, "I can forget to return a message to a staff member, or lose track of time and miss a planned observation of a teacher. But if I don't create and distribute in advance the special all-school assembly or testing bell schedule, that's really screwing up." In reality, little things do mean a great deal to the staff. The smooth management of routine tasks is one of the assistant principal's main jobs and the means by which the assistant principal is most likely to quickly earn or lose staff respect and trust.

Staff members need to trust and respect the assistant principal and believe that those feelings are mutual. Assistant principals need to be excellent listeners and hear people out, especially when staff is most frustrated. Often teachers just need to vent. But in some situations they go to the assistant principal with a student problem and expect the assistant principal to do what they want, which often is not ultimately in the best interests of the student. A frustrated teacher will demand the maximum consequence for student behavior, particularly when it is the tenth time the student has been late or mouthed off in class. The assistant principal needs to acknowledge that frustration but also help the staff member understand that while they will listen to what happened and what the staff member wants as followup, that is not necessarily what is going to happen. The smart assistant principal explains why. Teachers need to understand that when the assistant principal doesn't do precisely what they want her to do, it does not mean they have not been heard or supported. Teachers may be angry that a student was not suspended and instead given detention and a parent called, but it is not the teacher's job to determine the consequences. Assistant principals need to understand the frustration the staff member may be feeling but also to balance what happened with the needs of the student, within reason. Teaching can be an isolating profession and most teachers aren't privy to big-picture issues. Without being condescending, it is the job of the assistant principal to guide and explain decisions so the teacher feels validated, even if a compromise is appropriate. Lastly, it is imperative for the assistant principal to support the teacher in front of parents and students, but recognize that support can come in many forms. An assistant principal can let a parent know that a teacher was following school policy, but in an administrative role there is often the ability to make a different determination based on a broader scope of information. The assistant principal who can walk the fine line of demonstrating support yet compromise appropriately has mastered the art of administration.

Implementing the Principal's Vision: Do You See What I See?

Increasingly, school staff needs an assistant principal who fulfills the traditional management role, but also embraces the role of the educational leader. As the job of the school-based administrator becomes more demanding, assistant principals are increasingly called upon to serve in other complex roles; as an extension of the principal in articulating his vision, as a curricular or instructional leader, as a collaborator with other school-based leaders on strategic initiatives, and as a facilitator of institutional change. As with many of the roles the assistant principal assumes, their success depends on the guidance, positioning and accountability they have from their own leader—the principal mentor.

A key leadership function an assistant principal can demonstrate for the staff is to provide clarity while reinforcing the principal's vision, goals, and ideas. Because of the demands placed on the principal's time, staff members may be more likely to dialogue about plans and details and have routine questions answered by the assistant principal.

An example is the high-stakes state testing program that became required for graduation. The principal set a clear expectation that all senior students working to pass these tests would indeed graduate. The principal met with the assistant principal and fleshed out the basic resources that were available and what was and was not possible with the master schedule. From there, the assistant principal became the point of contact with the chief school instructional stakeholders on this project. He reiterated and explained the shared vision the principal has established, but worked with the other instructional leaders to establish the specific systems to implement the test preparation program. The assistant principal provided frequent updates for the principal, but the detail work was carried out by a collaborative group led by the assistant principal. In this case, the leadership demonstrated by the assistant principal extended beyond doing the actual work, to empowering stakeholders and overseeing the implementation of the plan.

Obviously this situation required a healthy degree of trust between the principal and the assistant principal. The positive result was that the assistant principal became an extension of the principal, using the principal's position power appropriately with the staff and executing the basic goal related to all students' graduation. When invoking the principal's name (i.e., "What the principal really wants us to do is...."), the assistant principal needs to be on very firm ground that this, indeed, is what the principal wants to have happen. By the same token, the assistant principal should not use the position authority of the principal as the sole means to lead the staff. Good ideas stand on their own merits, and strong assistant principals are able to design solutions that respect the principal's goals, but which are also aligned with their own leadership style.

Follow the (Instructional) Leader: What Does the Data Tell Us?

Another important role the assistant principal increasingly fulfills for the staff is of instructional leadership. High-stakes testing, national standards, ever-changing curriculum implementation, and district mandates all require assistant principals to lead in driving innovation and ensuring progress. In the ever-increasing data-driven world, schools are bombarded with information about student performance. The assistant principal must work with other school-based leaders to establish an understanding of how to access and interpret data. Leading structured departmental or team data chats effectively allow teachers to become knowledgeable about using data effectively to drive instruction.

The assistant principal is also charged with reviewing data with teachers and often having courageous conversations when the data is not positive. One assistant principal found alarming information when he reviewed the data of a particular department. An analysis he did showed that 68% of one teacher's students had a D or failed her class, as compared to 32% of another teacher's students. He did a departmental analysis and met with all of the teachers but removed teacher names from the data. The reality was most teachers knew which data was theirs. The one teacher was in denial and got very angry, claiming she had the more challenging students in her classes. Following some heated discussions with her peers, the teacher was ready to listen. The assistant principal was then able to work with the teacher to get to the root cause of the problem and help her make positive strides in student achievement. To the credit of both the assistant principal and the teacher, they worked well together and in a year's time, the turnaround in the teacher was remarkable. Making student data from classroom observations and grade analysis the focus of conferences allowed the teacher and assistant principal to define what is really meant by "continuous professional improvement" and ultimately improve student achievement.

Although it may be unnerving for a teacher to have the assistant principal frequently stopping by to catch part of a lesson, what good teacher doesn't want to be seen in action? Informal observation represents one of the best opportunities for the two to establish an ongoing dialogue about teaching and learning. Some call this "leadership by walking around," but for the teacher, it demonstrates a level of commitment the assistant principal has to understanding how the teacher works and what the teacher does well. For the assistant principal, it allows her to exercise one of an assistant principal's most important functions as an educational leader: accountability. While other school-based leaders, such as department chairs, team leaders, and staff development instructors all may have a hand in assisting teachers in becoming more effective, it is the school-based administrators who hold teachers accountable.

Collaboration Beyond "Playing Well with Others"

Closely aligned with instructional leadership is the assistant principal's role as a collaborator. Educational collaboration can take many shapes, but in relation to the staff, the assistant principal has two important roles: collaborator as a "doer" and collaborator as a "facilitator." As a "doer," the assistant principal is sometimes one among equals on a team of staff members.

In one example, a large high school was applying for a federal grant to create smaller learning communities. A collaborative writing team of seven teachers and supporting staff was assembled to gather data and write the necessary proposal. Although the assistant principal was charged with leading the team, her primary role was to write a particular section of the grant. The entire grant committee was successful, in part, because the assistant principal did not use mandates or her position power with the group. While she coordinated the overall process, she focused primarily on the one section and being one of many "doers." For many assistant principals this comes naturally, as many good assistant principals made a name for themselves as a leader by example or work ethic.

Perhaps more challenging is for the assistant principal to collaborate with the staff effectively as the "facilitator." Success in this area is defined in several key ways: assembling the right mix of people; promoting effective communication; "breaking logjams"; and giving credit to others. One assistant principal was charged with creating a work group to examine how students were admitted to honors-level classes. The most important collaborative decision the assistant principal made in this process was the composition of the group, to include people with various viewpoints, content area backgrounds, experience levels, and of different races and genders. At one point, the work group was split about a particular recommendation and the assistant principal, who was not a regular participant in the meetings, intervened. In recalling the situation, she reflected, "The most important thing I did was to keep my opinions about what I thought the outcome should be to myself, and instead drew their attention back to what the group had defined as the goal, and what the considerations were in their decision. They ultimately made the choice and broke their own logjam. My job was not to make a decision, but to ease them toward their own decision." In the end, the assistant principal was also quick to give the work group public praise to the staff as a whole for having resolved the issue. This win-win scenario came about because the assistant principal was focused on empowering others, rather than being the "doer," making the key decision herself. She was also quick to point out that this was not her natural tendency but only happened because the principal gently cautioned her at several points to "resist being the doer, instead frame the picture for them."

Like Most Things, It's the Relationship

If they are to have a good working relationship, the assistant principal must establish and cultivate trusting relationships with staff from the beginning. It is difficult for some assistant principals to understand that their role isn't to be a teacher's friend, but to be a safe person for staff to vent, discuss, and collaborate with, where confidentiality is honored. This can be a difficult balancing act if the assistant principal has risen through the ranks within a school and finds that he now supervises colleagues who were once his peers. Professional trust needs to be established and staff members must be confident that the assistant principal is treating them respectfully, has their best interests at heart, and is not looking to escalate or personalize conflicts that may arise.

In the final analysis, the assistant principal cannot ignore the need from the staff to "make the trains run on time." The task management decisions that the assistant principal makes are important and are the yardstick by which most assistant principals are measured by their colleagues. But the real gauge of effective leadership rests with finding the means to get others to focus on the goal, defining the task, nurturing collaboration, and sometimes hardest of all, stepping out and allowing others to do the job or define the solution.

5

The Assistant Principal Role: What the Parents and Community Need

It's about knowing the best thing to say after, "Hello, this is the assistant principal and I'm calling about your child."

Assistant principals are very familiar with the responsibility of working with parents and members of the school community. As a teacher, one learns the challenge of communicating with adults who have various parenting styles and who advocate in different ways for their child. As an assistant principal, a significant challenge is breaking down the intricacies of the learning process or a student's academic and behavioral strengths and needs for a parent. In addition, the courageous conversation with the parent of a child who is struggling can be difficult. Of the three primary educational constituency groups for educators—students, staff, and parents—the latter frequently can be the most unpredictable and the one that requires the most skill to manage effectively.

A Conversation with a Parent Is Rarely a One-on-One Proposition

For an assistant principal, developing positive relationships with parents and community members is the recognition that your work with them must represent the school's vision, culture, and policies, rather than your personal viewpoints. Working with parents cannot be an impersonal process, but rather, as one assistant principal describes it, "the parent and I are rarely the only two players in the game." It also requires the recognition that you are "the school" or "they" in decision making, as in, "The school says students must be present at the graduation rehearsal in order to participate in the ceremony" or "Seniors who don't attend school on Friday will not be excused." Although the assistant principal is implementing school policy, they may be viewed as "the enemy" and find themselves in confrontational situations with parents.

It is important to recognize that parent interactions rarely take place in isolation. Face it—parents talk among themselves, with their child, and with their children's friends. Interactions at the grocery store, the neighborhood pool, or church, or even comments overheard when a parent is driving a carpool, can make their way into a conversation an assistant principal has with a parent about an unrelated issue. Parents may tell the assistant principal information with complete certainty that it is fact, yet often it is their child's opinion. An interaction with one parent may actually have the effect of an interaction with many parent groups, just as positively meeting the needs of a member of the business community may pay dividends with many community groups, or vice versa.

The Assistant Principal as Community Organizer

One parent told an assistant principal that his son was disgusted that there was a specific area of the school where students were using drugs and that the school knew about it and made a conscious decision to look the other way. The parent proceeded to make this claim publicly at a parent meeting and actually threatened to go to the press with this information. The assistant principal apprised the principal of the situation immediately and they developed a plan for dealing with this parent as well as with his child. The reality was that there had been drug issues the previous year in the area the parent referred to but it had absolutely been addressed and that area was now the regular post for a member of the security team. There had been no issues since it was addressed and the student report was grossly inaccurate.

The assistant principal invited the parent in to meet with him and offered to take him on a school tour, which included the referenced area. He further invited the parent to drop in any time and visit that area. He also called for the student, and while not refuting the student's claim, asked him if he ever witnessed any drug activity or smelled anything to discretely make him aware so it could be dealt with. The student became sheepish and indicated that perhaps he had exaggerated the situation to his father but told the assistant principal he would let him know if he witnessed anything in the future. Because the assistant principal was proactive and nonconfrontational with both the parent and student, the issue, in fact, became a nonissue.

Sometimes assistant principals are called upon to mediate a conflict between students and their parents when issues escalate into the community. Handled sensitively and successfully, this can build all-important credibility for the assistant principal. For this reason, assistant principals should not look at parent contact as an isolated occurrence but should invite and welcome the parents' perspective in working out solutions involving their child. Parents can be valuable allies and usually appreciate being part of any process that involves the safety and well-being of their child.

It is important for assistant principals to process situations with another administrator, as this will produce decisions that are consistent within the school. This ensures the parent feels that the administration is "on the same page," as well as reasonable and fair in their decision making. Decisions made in isolation, or as snap judgments, sometimes in anger and without weighing all options, often come back to bite the assistant principal.

The Most Important Question Concerning Parents

What exactly do parents want? There are simple and not-so-simple answers to that question. The simple answer is that they want the best educational opportunities for their child, they want their child treated fairly, they want to feel respected, and they want to feel well-served by the school. A not-so-simple answer is much more complex. First, parents are attempting to navigate the vast and complicated bureaucracy of school. They are looking for answers, direction, and clarification. Although administrators are not the "Help Desk," they are frequently viewed as the keeper of all-important knowledge. Like it or not, it is a role they should embrace. Frequently, parents are trying to resolve conflicts between students, between students and teachers, between themselves and teachers, and even larger community issues. The assistant principal becomes the logical mediator, but needs to tread very carefully in what can become a tricky minefield.

When parents need to interact with an assistant principal, they are often angry and frustrated. A frustrated parent is often looking for someone to blame, particularly if their child is failing academically or in frequent trouble. That frustration is often taken out on the assistant principal, which can be painful and difficult to deal with. The key concept the assistant principal needs to remember in this situation is that parents are often angry because they love their child and they feel helpless. It is the responsibility of the assistant principal to help the student and parent in the most appropriate way.

How the assistant principal delivers bad news, may set the stage for their relationship with the parent. One assistant principal reflected that her own son's suspension from school taught her more about parent interactions than all of her other training and experiences. Prior to that event, she was mechanical when she delivered bad news, never taking into account how devastating that news would be to the parent. Her own experience made her far more empathetic and understanding of what the parent on the other end of the phone was going through and it ultimately made her a better administrator.

Occasionally, parents, knowingly or unknowingly, are looking for advice from administrators on how to best parent their children. An assistant principal who calls a parent about their child's suspension might end up giving advice on how the parent can make that time out of school productive and reinforce the underlying lesson behind the suspension. This is appropriate, but needs to be approached cautiously. One assistant principal sees it this way: "They may ask for my advice, but it doesn't mean they'll always take it or like it." Lastly, believe it or not, sometimes what parents want is "nothing." They simply want to express their frustrations, say their piece and be done. These parents just need to believe they are heard. Often they are far more frustrated by their child's behaviors than the assistant principal could possibly be.

Why Don't Parents Come with an Instruction Manual?

There are a number of general "dos and don'ts" that assistant principals should consider when working with parents and trying to address their needs. The first involves asking the most basic of questions: What do they want? Are they requesting information, or assistance or is this one of those times when they don't really want anything but an ear? One assistant principal has what she calls her "$64,000 Question." In her words, "I always make it a point to listen first, sometimes for an extended period of time. If it's not clear to me, as respectfully as possible I eventually pose the question: 'What is it you're seeking today?" or "How can I help you?" It's amazing how often that puts a pregnant pause in the conversation, helps to lessen the emotion, encourages the parent to put the main issue out there, and, most importantly, allows us to move forward in a productive manner."

Another best practice is to do your homework where the parent and family are concerned. This is where the principal, counselor, or a fellow assistant principal can serve as a valuable source of information. They may have a relationship with the family, or have worked with an older sibling. It cannot be overestimated how understanding family dynamics can play a productive role in meeting a parent's needs and solving problems.

In today's world of divorce, remarriage, and blended families, one assistant principal has an important piece of advice: know the parent's correct name. As he puts it, "I never assume that a student and her father have the same last name, and before I ever pick up the phone, I confirm through records or with the student what her dad's name is. It's hard to build a relationship when, in my first words I've made the most basic mistake by calling the parent by the wrong name." Another tip is to pull up any pertinent information about the student before returning or making a call; grades, attendance, previous disciplinary infractions, anything that helps paint a picture of the whole student. Many school districts have databases with student pictures; it is critical that the assistant principal know who the child is before calling a parent.

There are also a number of "don'ts" for assistant principals to avoid in their work with parents. Don't attempt to solve problems that are not yours to solve. Parents will often "go to the top" in seeking a solution or answers for their child. Often their first call is to the principal, which may be delegated and returned by the grade-level assistant principal. In large schools, the assistant principal can't possibly have detailed knowledge of every academic requirement or every situation. Similarly, an assistant principal doesn't always have details of a conflict between a student and a teacher. In these instances, rather than attempting to solve a problem it's far more productive to pose the question, "Have you spoken to the teacher about this issue?" Amazingly, many parents have not. Or if they have and have not gotten the response they are looking for, it is often more appropriate for them to speak next with a team leader, department head, or counselor who is more familiar with the issue, the considerations, and how similar problems have previously been solved. It's important not to circumvent the chain of command.

If the assistant principal doesn't have enough information to assess the situation, rather than making a snap judgment to resolve the issue, a golden phrase may be, "I need to look into this situation; I'll get back to you by the end of the day." The assistant principal may have a good answer, but it may not be the best answer without complete information. This is sometimes difficult, because administrators are, by nature, problem-solvers. But one assistant principal puts it best: "I strive to be helpful first and quick second."

Difficult Conversations: Is the Glass Half Empty or Half Full?

A final consideration relates to the interpersonal dynamic between assistant principals and parents. If a parent calls or stops by primarily to vent, sometimes this is just "required listening." When an assistant principal's solution to solving this problem is to shut the parent down or avoid listening to what the parent is actually saying, the assistant principal may miss an important opportunity to listen, read between the lines, and decipher what the parent may actually be looking for. Sometimes it's just a matter of going in with the proper mindset. One assistant principal frames the issue this way: "I try hard not to lose sight of the fact that they're really more frustrated with their child than they are with me." Most effective principals are deft at "talking angry parents off the ledge." Assistant principals need to take the time to talk through specific situations with their principal and then discuss productive ways to deal with negative parent interactions. Better yet, the assistant principal should ask to observe a meeting between the principal and a difficult parent. There is an art to redirecting negative parent energy and most principals are likely a master of this skill.

Difficult phone conversations present a particular challenge for assistant principals. As much as they would like to be considered instructional leaders first and foremost, it is often a primary role of assistant principals to deal with discipline issues and make a difficult call to the parent. Begin with clearly identifying yourself and the reason you've called. Put them at ease, as much as possible: "I'm calling because I need to let you know that your son was in a fight at lunch today. I want you to know that he's okay and sitting here beside me." "I need to talk with you about an unpleasant situation with your daughter here at school that I hope we can work together to make right." It doesn't change the facts of the situation, but sets a positive tone.

After speaking initially, allow the parent to digest the situation. It is then important to listen carefully and answer all of the parent's questions. The assistant principal should be patient but clear about why they are calling. One veteran assistant principal summarized it this way: "I don't pick up the phone until I've truly asked and answered three questions in my mind: What are going to be the parent's concerns? What's the best possible outcome for this situation? What are some possible things that I and the parent can do together to get us there?"

Positive Parent Communication: The Glass is Full!

Although the difficult interaction with parents is stressful, there are also numerous proactive opportunities that assistant principals have to forge positive relationships with parents. Being proactive in situations and alerting parents before something becomes an issue is appreciated by most parents. Parents also appreciate when the assistant principal takes the time to call when something good happens. A call that begins with, "I just wanted to tell you what a great job your son did today when he *(fill in the blank)*." Parents greatly appreciate when the assistant principal has good news to share, particularly when a student previously has had negative issues in school.

With many opportunities to develop positive relationships with parents, the principal plays a key-mentoring role. Principals can encourage assistant principals to write informative pieces for newsletters, the school website, and professional publications, all which build credibility for the assistant principal. An update on an instructional initiative that the assistant principal is coordinating allows the community to see them as an instructional leader. This also allows the assistant principal to refine and highlight her written communication skills.

Parent organization meetings and forums are perfect opportunities for assistant principals to present and analyze school-related data and corresponding improvement plans. While being the administrator on duty at a school concert or sporting event may seem like just another night out in a long line of required evening activities, it also represents an opportunity. Assistant principals can use this time to interact with parents about positive student achievements, help answer challenging questions, and solicit parent involvement on school programs. The principal is the main portal to the parent community, but an assistant principal with the right training, skills, and positioning can also build important positive credibility that translates into parent support for the school and school community.

6

Hey! What About What I Need? And How Do I Know This?

After attending to students, staff, and parents, what's missing? Every administrator has a unique set of professional and personal needs that require attention for growth.

Examining Both Sides of the Equation: Personal and Professional Needs

Effective assistant principals recognize that after they have taken care of everyone around them at school, there are things that they need as well, and that's okay. From a professional standpoint, there are obvious needs that begin with a development plan that takes into account their strengths and challenges as a professional. But professional needs don't end with a formalized professional development timeline. In fact, if you polled most assistant principals and asked them what they needed from the professional workplace to do their job more effectively, the list would probably include a number of intangibles, such as the specifics of their administrative assignment, how and if they are positioned for success, the support they receive, and the consideration their ideas are given by others. But most importantly, an assistant principal needs a principal invested in the assistant principal's growth and development, a principal who is willing to be a role model of professionalism.

Each assistant principal has a distinct set of personal needs that must be addressed for them to be most effective in their career. Sometimes it's about the time and space they need to meet family or personal needs. Other times it's more about recognizing and respecting other commitments they make outside the workplace. It's also about the need to get along with your workmates on a personal level. Most administrators welcome a colleague they can vent to and laugh with at the end of the day. Every assistant principal needs a trusted colleague to ask for advice, a supportive significant other, and a critical friend; someone to give them a kick in the butt when it's warranted. Regardless of what the need may be, the role of the assistant principal requires a tremendous commitment of time, mental focus, and physical energy. Because this represents a balancing act, the less anxiety an administrator feels about integrating their personal and professional life, the more content and effective they are in the job. Each assistant principal's needs and circumstances are unique. Truly effective principals work to recognize and honor the "little things" that are important to their team members.

The professional needs of the assistant principal should always begin with an ongoing development plan. Professional development training is inescapable in education, but it doesn't have to be strictly obligatory. The assistant principal should view district training mandates as minimums, not as an ending point, and recognize that it is not necessarily oriented to what the assistant principal needs specifically to develop their professional skills. To truly address their individual needs, assistant principals should consider a professional skill inventory, found on many educational association websites and available from other professional development organizations. The value of a standardized inventory assessment is that it provides objective information about one's skill gaps as an administrator and ideas about a development plan. Left to their own devices, assistant principals rarely tackle training in the areas in which they are most uncomfortable. One assistant principal's take was this: "I knew data-driven decision making was a growing expectation in our work, and I spent far too much time avoiding it because it's so complicated."

Experience (and the Experience of Others) Is the Best Teacher

In addition to formalized experiences, the best training an assistant principal can get is the job-embedded training that occurs doing day-to-day tasks that help make a school run effectively. Every task an assistant principal faces can be viewed through the lens of professional development. Even mundane day-to-day tasks can be addressed in a way that makes them more interesting and a professional growth experience. For instance, every assistant principal is charged with a variety of scheduling tasks, whether it is creating the master schedule, a testing schedule, a bell schedule or even scheduling observations of teachers they supervise. A task this tedious can actually be a model for continuous improvement.

In a well-run team, assistant principals work with and effectively mentor their peers so that what worked and what can be improved upon is a part of an ongoing process and conversation. In this same example, one assistant principal might begin the process of drafting the schedule, sit down with the other assistant principals and throw out a series of questions: "What works and what are possible pitfalls?" "What if…?" "Would it be better if…?" Who benefits if we…?" When you gather two or more team members for informal brainstorming, you automatically assemble a variety of experiences, lessons learned, and sets of eyes and ears. The value of this synergy is obvious but often in the name of "getting it off our plate" administrative teams don't often enough take the opportunity to creatively problem solve and learn from each other. Comparing how different people approach tasks can assist each member of the team in refining their own skills and in developing a better product. For the lone assistant principal in a school, a colleague at another school, a lead teacher, a counselor, or the principal may be good sources of the same experience. The point is to talk a task through with others when trying to improve on a process.

But what do assistant principals need in order to maximize this type of collaboration? In short, they need to be able to build and contribute to a workplace where their ideas are listened to and given consideration by others. Even if what they are suggesting isn't possible or practical, assistant principals must feel free to express ideas in a collaborative environment where they feel respected and valued. Often assistant principals have fabulous ideas, yet are quickly stifled if what they suggest is outside the norm. Before ideas are shot down, effective teams look at all aspects of the ideas and make decisions collectively about whether an idea has merit and is worth trying. Sometime highly effective practices are a result of seemingly harebrained ideas that are tweaked and given credence. Being flexible and willing to think outside of the box or established school norms can produce a more effective end result for any project or problem. But if the first impulse is to get into "that's not the way we do it here," the assistant principal will shut down and not offer opinions or suggestions, just as we see with students in the classroom. The flip side of this is the veteran assistant principal who scoffs at new ideas and stifles the process. Assistant principals need to keep an open mind and be willing to try new things, but if appropriate, be willing to go in a different direction. Schools, even highly effective schools rarely excel if the motto is "if it ain't broke...."

The Care and Feeding of an Assistant Principal

Beyond formal and informal learning experiences, much of what an assistant principal needs professionally falls into the category of "care and feeding"—how they are valued and treated and to what degree they are respected in the workplace. Assistant principals should have stimulating administrative assignments, yet not be overwhelmed. There is a delicate balance between an assignment that is a stretch for an assistant principal and one that is out of reach and ultimately frustrating. Assistant principals need to speak up and self-advocate but they also benefit from working with a principal who understands the big picture and truly has their best interests in mind. Some duties and assignments can feel like punishment if not explained by the principal why they need to be done or why a particular person has been charged with doing them.

One assistant principal did not want to oversee the high-stakes testing process required for graduation. His assistant principal colleague had skillfully led the process the previous year, and he didn't feel it was necessary to reassign this leadership challenge to him. It was only when the principal made the connection to his role as the 12th grade class administrator and ensuring that all students were prepared for graduation, that he understood the logical connection to this assignment.

Assistant principals have a professional need to be in the loop, to understand and have access to big-picture information. Principals need to be sure assistant principals are well versed on financial budgets, community concerns, and the most current educational issues. Effective principals request to bring assistant principals to administrative meetings whenever possible, even if on a rotating schedule. This exposure is helpful to assistant principals on a variety of levels. It allows them to "be seen" and affords them the opportunity to learn and be in the know about what is happening at the district level. For assistant principals who are considering applying for a principalship, attending meetings at the district level can provide valuable networking that is just not possible in the isolation of a school.

A final issue of "care and feeding" in the administrative setting is an important one: Assistant principals need to be able to take some risks even if it means they make mistakes. But if the professional environment that is created has no margin for error or risk taking on the part of the assistant principal, then there will be a pattern of continual anxiety and disappointment. No administrator is perfect. With dozens of decisions made daily, even the most skilled veteran makes some bad decisions. The key may well be what the principal and assistant principal do as a result of their decision. Sometimes it's a matter of the two closing the door, processing what happened, and determining what could have been done differently. Other times, when the mistake is more public, the principal should encourage the assistant principal to make amends equally as publically. Conversely, good principals recognize in the same situation that the assistant principal does not need to be "thrown under the bus" to learn a lesson, but instead be shielded from criticism. As a result, the principal may take the heat for the decision on themselves, providing the kind of support that many assistant principals find most important.

You Can't Take Care of Others If You Don't Take Care of Yourself

As important as the professional considerations, the assistant principal needs to carefully assess what personal supports he needs to be effective at his job. Assistant principals spend a lot of time taking care of the needs of others. They work closely with student issues, hold parents' hands, soothe crying new teachers, become a sounding board to people at a variety of levels, and the list goes on and on. At the end of the day, it can be positively exhausting to deal with everyone's issues, leaving the assistant principal worn out and emotionally drained. Principals need to remember that assistant principals have lives and families and there needs to be a reasonable balance with job demands and allowing for personal time.

One principal insisted that every single sporting event be covered by an assistant principal. The assistant principals at that school were covering literally hundreds of events where in many cases an athletic director was fully equipped to handle any issues. Certainly, events with a large attendance need a significant amount of coverage, but this principal demanded that events where there had never been issues (such as tennis matches and some junior varsity sports) have administrative coverage. The assistant principals in that school were so exhausted and resentful that they could not function as a team and one by one requested to be moved to another school where the workload expectations were more reasonable, manageable, and in line with district norms.

In another situation, a female assistant principal with young children greatly appreciated when her principal understood the importance of events for her children, such as the annual elementary school Halloween parade. His response was always that as long as she had her responsibilities covered at school, she could go. This family friendly attitude ensured that the assistant principal was extremely grateful and less guilt-ridden as a working mother. She ultimately worked far longer hours and brought her children to many events at the school, even when she was not officially on duty.

Principals also need to recognize that assistant principals need time for medical appointments, personal fitness, and health, as well as occasionally the "pursuit of happiness." Administrators work long hours and it is virtually impossible to schedule doctor or dental appointments that do not conflict with the workday. Principals need to understand and make sure their assistant principals do not miss important appointments that can impact their health and well-being for the sake of attendance at yet another meeting. Scheduling time to exercise ultimately helps improve the outlook of assistant principals and the productivity of the school.

One assistant principal very comfortably justified her Tuesday–Thursday after-school workout routine as sacred: "If I don't get to work out, not only am I not as good for my kids at school, but I'm no good to my family at home." Another assistant principal enjoyed acting in community theatre, but found these opportunities rare with the weekly evening activities associated with being an assistant principal. When a particular show he had been itching to do was being cast, he asked his colleagues if they would trade and assume some of his duties for the 6-week rehearsal and performance schedule. Although it caused a temporary heavier load for the other assistant principals, they also knew how important it was to him and how happy it would make him. They also recognized that somewhere down the road, they probably would have a similar request of their own: an extended trip, once-in-a-lifetime travel adventure, or taking their own child on a college tour. What allows administrators to extend themselves or make allowances for their colleagues in this way is a simple recognition that there is a great deal beyond school that contributes to our happiness, well-being, and job satisfaction.

What assistant principals need to be successful in their job extends far beyond the obvious professional development and experience in the position. Principal mentors have a responsibility to help their assistant principals chart a course professionally, and serve as an ongoing role model. But it is important for both the principal and the assistant principal to understand what is important and what makes the assistant principal tick on both a professional and a personal level so as to fundamentally meet their needs so they can meet the needs of others.

7

Principal and Assistant Principal Communication: The Honest High-Wire Act

Like a tightrope walker who balances many considerations, communication between a principal and assistant principal can be high risk, high reward. But the goal is always the same: to stay on the rope.

Walking the Walk

It is not unusual for principals and assistant principals to have issues with effective communication. Although our understanding of best practices related to effective communication is endless, how we in education "walk the walk" with our colleagues, students, and parents often leaves room for improvement.

When examining the typical principal–assistant principal relationship, there is usually a healthy respect between individuals, but often many things are left unspoken. An assistant principal may respect the position authority of his or her supervisor, but not always understand the underlying assumptions or rationale for the principal's decisions. A well-intended assistant principal may make a decision without the principal being in the loop, thereby minimizing the value of the otherwise effective decision. In the universe of decisions, information and input that flows between and around a principal and assistant principal serves as a daily test of their relationship. Like tightrope walkers, the principal and assistant principal are looking to balance a number of needs while still staying on the rope. Honest and effective communication practiced consistently minimizes the risk of someone falling off.

Effective communication can take many forms, including communication between the principal and assistant principal and communication with other stakeholders. Communication between the principal and assistant principal encompasses understanding the role each plays, establishing norms about what is said and not shared, and understanding the principal's vision and bottom-line expectations. Communication with other stakeholders includes how the principal mentors the assistant principal on clear communication with staff, students, and parents, how the assistant principal conveys the principal's vision, and avoiding triangulation with other stakeholders.

Metacognitive Processing: Was I Just Thinking That or Did I Say it Out Loud?

Most principals and assistant principals express an interest for an "open dialogue" with each other. Yet far fewer can articulate the practical steps both sides can take to make this happen. The first is for the principal to take a metacognitive approach to daily leadership—literally by thinking aloud about the decisions that the principal makes and providing a rationale for these decisions to the assistant principal. Better yet, the principal engages the assistant principal in discussing and problem solving how to deal with a particular issue. Good principals make numerous decisions on a daily basis and don't assume those around them always understand the reasons why certain decisions were made. In fact, the assistant principal benefits tremendously from hearing the reasoning behind sound decision making. One principal made a habit of beginning parent conferences about student suspensions with the sincere statement, "Let's figure out how we can get your child back into school successfully." Before one conference, the principal decided to include the assistant principal in the process and previewed it this way: "The first thing I say to the parent is the most important. If they understand that this meeting is about looking forward and not backward, it will be more productive. The parent also understands that we want the same thing; what is best for their child. This defuses parent anger and lays the groundwork for a more successful meeting." True to form, the conference was successful.

Afterward, the principal debriefed with the assistant principal about why, in her experience, this was a positive icebreaker for this type of meeting and was consistent with her personal philosophy. This put the parent at ease and allowed them to focus on what needed to change about the student's behavior. But the discussion about the "why" behind this statement was what promoted the open dialogue between the principal and assistant principal. Principals who make a habit of saying "I'm thinking about doing this because," "the reason we do this is," or "in making this decision I had to consider" truly give their assistant principal a window into their thinking. Likewise, assistant principals must become active listeners and ask their own metacognitive questions, such as, "Why did you say that?" or "What did you consider when you…?" to open the same window. Thinking about thinking produces better decisions and can promote discussion about a wide range of leadership scenarios.

Principals promote effective communication with their assistant principals when they consistently reference their ideas back to the vision and goals of the school—the big picture.

Assistant principals frequently work on specific school-management tasks, like an assembly schedule or one for observing a teacher. Some days their world has a very narrow focus. Principals tend to have a greater sense of the "big picture." In considering numerous decisions, they think in broader terms, including about the parents, the community at-large, district-level norms, and, most importantly, what is in the best interests of students. So while an assistant principal might see merit in scheduling a special assembly in the middle of the day because it fits well with the school schedule and all students can attend, the principal understands that having the assembly at night allows for students and parents to attend, as well as potential coverage from the local TV news. It becomes incumbent upon the principal to reference the impact of the big picture on a regular basis for the assistant principal. Likewise, when significant decisions need to be made, the assistant principal should touch base with the principal to ensure they haven't overlooked any "larger" considerations before charging ahead.

In the Loop, Part I: The Principal Never Like Surprises

Another important aspect of strong communication between a principal and assistant principal involves being kept "in the loop." Assistant principals often focus on detail work such as the action plans behind a school vision or goal. But as plans move forward, one of the main balancing acts becomes how much is too much information to share with the principal and how much is too little?

An assistant principal needed to create a plan to implement the state assessment test during the school day. He charged ahead with establishing room assignments, teacher proctors, and student assignments. He communicated with all of these groups, but left one person out of the equation—the principal. When the principal asked for status updates, the assistant principal consistently remarked confidently, "I've got it." The principal, trusted the assistant principal and left it at that. The night before the test was to be administered, the assistant principal brought the plans to the principal, who quickly spotted numerous flaws in the logistics. She started asking more questions, uncovering more problems. The assistant principal was demoralized and felt like he had failed miserably. The principal second-guessed herself, thinking she should have asked for more details along the way. They worked quickly, pulled in some additional resources, corrected the obvious problems and the testing occurred without a hitch. Although the situation was rectified, a small amount of trust was lost because the principal was not in the loop. It became an important learning experience for both the assistant principal and the principal.

One of the most important considerations for avoiding problems like this is seemingly simple; both sides need to work at basic formal and informal accountability. It can be as easy as the principal checking in with the assistant principal for updates when the state assessment test schedule was being planned, or the assistant principal shooting a brief e-mail that begins, "Just giving you an update…." Many assistant principals worry that they pop into their principal's office too frequently with mundane information. The reality is that it only becomes a bother when it leads to gaps in communication or consistently wastes time. One assistant principal describes his "secret solution" to this problem: "I keep a sticky pad on my desk just for the principal. Periodically throughout the day I'll make a brief notes on it, and once or twice a day I'll pop into her office when I sense it's convenient, beginning by saying, 'I'm just putting you in the loop on this.' I don't stay long, and usually the conversation is short. If my principal wants to ask me questions, great. If not, I disappear."

In the Loop, Part II: The Principal's Eyes and Ears

If the principal wants to remain in the loop then the principal needs to view time with the assistant principal as time well spent, regardless of how frequent or clock-consuming it may seem. President Franklin Roosevelt called First Lady Eleanor Roosevelt his "eyes and ears." Similarly, assistant principals are a logical extension of the principal's authority, vision, and goals for the school. Assistant principals see certain aspects of school life in greater detail than the principal, and provide insight that the principal might not otherwise have. A detailed conversation with an assistant principal might prove just as beneficial as if the principal had taken a well-timed stroll in the hallways. Truly honest conversation between the two takes time, but also allows the principal to ultimately understand their blind spot—the issue that the principal may not see.

Keeping the principal in the loop in emergency or unusual situations is critical, particularly when the principal is out of the building or behind closed doors. In one instance, the principal was in a meeting with an under-performing teacher when it was reported to the assistant principal that a student in the building may have a gun. The assistant principal did not alert the principal immediately and worked with school security to investigate the situation. In the meantime, rumors were rampant among students and one student called her father to report what she had heard. The parent called the school demanding to speak to the principal, and was told the principal was in a meeting. The parent then called the local media and the situation spun out of control—all while the principal had no idea what was going on. When the district supervisor called and the principal was clueless about what they were talking about, the event took an ugly turn. Although the principal may not have done anything differently than the assistant principal did, he was put in a compromising position just because he was not given timely information about a highly sensitive and potentially dangerous situation.

Honesty Never Fails

In the end, honest, open, and trusting communication between a principal and assistant principal usually develops over time, often through trial and error. Both parties need to work at valuing what the other has to offer while understanding that both may make mistakes. Nothing puts that high-wire balance to a greater test than having to admit that you made a big mistake.

One assistant principal inadvertently sent an inappropriate e-mail about a parent to the parent. The assistant principal sincerely recognized that he was wrong in writing the e-mail in the first place, and now was paralyzed with what to do. But over a period of years he had built a trusting communication relationship with his principal and he didn't hesitate. He walked into her office, showed her the e-mail. The assistant principal told her, "I need some advice. I'm mortified that this happened." The principal could have gone ballistic as she certainly knew the assistant principal knew better, but chose that moment to put emotion aside and mentor instead. "You fall on the sword, and you make a total and complete apology. You don't make excuses for your behavior, you promise to work tirelessly to make amends. And you take whatever consequences come your way." It was difficult advice, but true. But mostly, it was latest good example of a positive communicative relationship built over many years and experiences.

8

Assistant Principal Communication: How to Effectively Connect with Others

In the high-profile world of administration, what are the effective means to "win friends and influence people?"

One reason why many assistant principals are appointed to their positions is because they possess effective communication skills—they can write clearly and conference effectively with other professionals. Novice assistant principals soon discover that there are a whole host of conventions and considerations about administrative communication with parents, large staff groups, and the community. When mistakes are made on this broader level, the results are usually obvious to a wide array of people. This is a good reason for the principal to serve as an effective mentor to the assistant principal, and the assistant principal must to be open to constructive criticism. Conversely, the assistant principals need to ultimately develop an honest and open relationship with their principal so they can share their opinion when something did not go particularly well for the principal. In this case, the assistant principal must realize that this may be a difficult conversation or that it might not be an appropriate one to have.

Learning from "The Great Communicator"

The principal meets and corresponds daily with a seeming endless parade of students, staff, and parents, and has numerous opportunities to engage in effective communication with these groups. One assistant principal marveled at the way her principal would take the angriest parents behind closed doors, and emerge each time arm-in-arm with the parent with smiles all around. Finally, one day when there was another disgruntled parent on the principal's doorstep, she said, "I have to see you do this." The principal looked amused wondering what she meant. The assistant principal explained what she had observed time and again, and it dawned on the principal that this common scenario might be a teachable moment for the assistant principal. The assistant principal observed the meeting, and after the conference, the principal walked the assistant principal through what she had sensed about the issue, what she had listened for, how she chose her words—a graduate course in best practices. What actually happened in the conference was that the principal validated the parent's concerns while focusing on the student. The principal understood that the parent was frustrated and just knowing that the principal was willing to listen and then problem solve, made a big difference to this parent. But it was the assistant principal having the courage to ask, and the principal being open to modeling what was second nature to her, that became an important lesson for the assistant principal. Every day in a school brings a similar opportunity.

In addition, principals correspond via e-mail with parents, district-level personnel, and community officials every day. The high-quality responses that principals compose can easily be shared by blind copying or by forwarding to the assistant principal. This accomplishes many things. The principal models how he responds to specific issues and also keeps the assistant principal in the loop about the issues. One assistant principal had this take: "I learned more about how to run a school from reading my principal's responses to sticky e-mails that I couldn't even begin to answer. It was an art, but a learnable art. It was an exercise in risk taking and trust to share it with us, but it was training I wouldn't have gotten otherwise."

The Risks of Putting It Out There

Assistant principals need to be open to having their principal mentors or other colleagues critique or provide input on nonroutine written correspondence. One assistant principal who valued his principal's input characterized it this way: "My principal is not my copyeditor. She doesn't correct my grammar or my mechanics so much as she considers the tone, the message, and whether I've addressed the issue at hand." Indeed, many assistant principals believe that running a draft of a letter to a parent, a newsletter article, or a response to a staff concern by their principal is the same as running a spell check—you automatically do it. "I know I'm an effective writer, in general," one assistant principal explained, "but my principal or another one of my assistant-principal colleagues almost always catches a part of the equation that I've missed. My rule is at least two sets of eyes for the important things." It requires trust and sometimes admitting fallibility, especially if the input is from a fellow assistant principal. But most assistant principals would likely admit that communicating effectively is more important than issues of pride or ego.

Principals take a risk when they provide opportunities for their assistant principal to be front and center with written correspondence and presentations within the school community. This opportunity can instill confidence in the assistant principal when it goes well. It can take the form of a newsletter article to parents about a particular program that the assistant principal is spearheading, speaking at a student forum and welcoming guests to an evening activity, conducting a question and answer night for parents new to the community, or doing the morning announcements. Assistant principals need to be in the habit of running difficult correspondence and public addresses through their principal or at least another trusted, veteran assistant principal. The input or changes may be minor, but usually reflect experience and the "big picture" vision on the part of the principal.

An assistant principal recounted the story of an e-mail he was prepared to send out, certain that it was accurate. Still, realizing that it would only take an additional minute or two to have someone else look it over, he forwarded it to another experienced assistant principal. The veteran assistant principal immediately raced to the assistant principal's office pointing out that he was inadvertently divulging confidential student information. It bears repeating: Most administrators are effective writers, but all administrator benefit from a second (or third) set of eyes for written communication.

...And Speaking of E-mail

Decades ago, the telephone was the primary mode of communication with parents for administrators. This was a time-consuming and often frustrating process, particularly when playing "phone tag" and having attempts at immediate communication drag on for days. In addition, once the problem was identified and discussed, there usually needed to be additional followup calls and, often, meetings.

Through the years, e-mail has evolved to be a primary form of communication for administrators. This is a mixed blessing as the rate of communication has sharply increased as has the time administrators have to address the magnitude of e-mail they receive. Often issues that would not warrant a phone call from parents are transferred to an e-mail, or to many e-mails. The immediacy of e-mail also lengthens the administrator's day as there is an expectation that they will respond immediately, regardless of the time of day. Getting control of this potential monster is a critical skill for assistant principals.

E-mail can often bring out the worst in people and the assistant principal needs to think long and hard before responding to an angry or negative e-mail. Taking time to walk away from an e-mail draft that was written in response to an angry e-mail can help prevent exacerbating a situation. In addition, sometimes copying the principal on difficult communication can accomplish several things, including letting the parent know that the principal is aware of the situation, which can serve to scale back the parent's anger. People use e-mail to vent and even to bully. It is important for assistant principals to not take things personally and to recognize when they are dealing with raw frustration.

The number one rule, when replying to an e-mail is to check who is copied on the reply. Many times replying to everyone is inappropriate. By the same token, never respond in what could be considered an inappropriate way, as you never know who might see it.

One assistant principal received an e-mail from a teacher complaining about how a situation was handled. The assistant principal was extremely frustrated by this and thought he was replying to the other administrators who were copied on her e-mail. He vented his frustration and said some pretty harsh and unprofessional things about the teacher, not realizing he had copied her on his response. The teacher was angry and hurt and the assistant principal had to work very hard to reestablish trust with her. He fell on the sword, apologized profusely, and worked very hard to make amends. It was a significant learning experience for the assistant principal. Ironically, the teacher made a similar mistake with a parent, which made her far more understanding of the assistant principal's gaff.

E-mail often has a tone or edge that may not be evident in a meeting or conversation. When it becomes apparent that nothing is being accomplished through e-mail, this is the time the assistant principal needs to pick up the phone and communicate directly with the sender. One assistant principal abided by a simple personal rule: If he hasn't resolved an issue after trading three e-mail messages, he picks up the phone. Very often the personal touch can speak volumes and issues can be resolved amicably and expeditiously.

E-mail can also be used in a very positive way. In some communities, parents make a point of e-mailing the principal or assistant principal when they want to commend a staff member. Printing the e-mail for the staff member's file and thanking the sender reinforces this positive behavior and increases the likelihood it will happen again.

Assistant principals may use a school internal folder as a way to communicate on many levels. In some schools, use of this folder helps with a green initiative as hard copies of information are reduced. Bell schedules, roosters, absence lists, field trips, special programs, and other information may be updated regularly and help keep everyone in the loop with what is happening in the school. This is also a perfect vehicle to commend and recognize staff. It is extremely important, however, to have the folder administrator be able to delete deliberately or inadvertently posted inappropriate messages.

Just as parents communicate with administrators regularly through e-mail, so do students. Students often will e-mail a question or request if they have a comfort level with the assistant principal. By the same token, when the e-mail address does not make it obvious who the sender is, crank or inappropriate e-mail may be more prevalent.

Administrators Sometimes Need Extended Time, Too

The secret to success in communication with others may be a question of having enough time to do the job right. On a given day, most assistant principals receive numerous e-mails and phone calls, and have staff, students, and parents stopping by their office. The constant stop/start disjointed nature of the position is a universal constant in education. Out of sheer necessity, administrators strive to be efficient in their communication, make quick decisions, and try to stay ahead of this daily avalanche. Much of our work-related communication can be dispatched quickly. But the reality is that not all forms of communication fall into the same category. At times, a situation or issue requires what is becoming an old-fashioned notion in our increasingly fast-paced, instant-results-and-response-oriented world—time, reflection, and consideration. If a parent calls with a concern about his or her child, sometimes it is best to say, "I need to talk to the teacher and gather some more information. Can I call you back no later than tomorrow morning?" If a teacher stops in an assistant principal's office unexpectedly with a complex problem, it's not a bad thing to say, "I need to think about that and get back to you." Because a parent has sent three e-mails in rapid succession does not mean there must be three immediate responses. As mentioned before, it is not a good thing for an assistant principal to be swayed more by a desire to be quick and decisive, than to be reflective and thoughtful. In these situations is a good practice set a timeframe for when the assistant principal will get back to the other person.

What does this extra time afford? For starters, it provides the opportunity to gather more information and talk through a solution with a colleague. It can also give the assistant principal time to really consider the issue when they've stepped away from the daily barrage of activity. One administrator's guiding principle in this area was simple: "I make much better and sometimes different important decisions once I sleep on a problem. Twelve or 24 hours later can make a big difference." Indeed, many assistant principals value their spouse or significant other to be an objective sounding board when formulating a communication in response to a problem without obvious answers. A final word in this area: If a teacher, parent, or student requires immediate approval when more time is probably necessary to understand the true issue, then the immediate answer should probably be "no." Within reasonable boundaries, the assistant principal has the discretion to determine the timeliness of the response.

Please Don't Put Me In the Middle of This

Another consideration in communication with others is recognizing the pitfalls of triangulation. Like a child will sometimes go to the parent they believe will give the child the most favorable answer, staff will sometimes do this, too. One assistant principal recalled the time the music teacher casually stopped by to toss out the idea of a potential field trip, ending with, "What do you think of the idea?" Just as casually, the assistant principal replied that he thought the idea had merit. Two weeks later, the principal asked the assistant principal why he had approved the music field trip that was the same day as a previously scheduled school assembly. The assistant principal offered that he had not approved the trip, only that he thought it was a good idea. The principal related that the music teacher had claimed the assistant principal had approved the trip, knowing full well that the principal would not approve—classic triangulation.

When staff or students are seeking approval, it doesn't take much to add the phrase, "that's a good idea, but let me check with the principal," or "I don't think that's going to be a problem, but why don't you run it by the principal," or "that's not a decision I can make, you need to speak with the principal." Likewise, principals will often recognize that they don't have to have all the answers, sending staff to their assistant principal with phrases such as, "You know the assistant principal is spearheading that plan, he knows more about it than me," or "I'm okay with it, but make sure the assistant principal is onboard," or "If the assistant principal can make it work, go for it."

With Great Power Comes Great Responsibility

A final aspect of communication that assistant principals should consider is how they use the principal's position authority with other people. By design, assistant principals are often informally and formally the principal's designee. Some even serve as acting principal in the principal's absence. But in the most informal sense, most principals expect assistant principals to make similar decisions and communicate as they would, keeping to their own philosophy, stated expectations or vision for the school. In most cases, this is for a good reason: the buck stops with the principal, and they are accountable for consequences of school decisions. In many instances, the use of the principal's position power can be a good thing.

One assistant principal recalled getting an e-mail from a department chair who was attempting to give a glowing recommendation for a mediocre teacher with the hopes of "moving him on." The assistant principal knew (and agreed) with the principal's philosophy of always being truthful when another school was asking for a recommendation, despite the fact that it might rid their school of a problem employee. The assistant principal responded privately to the department chair with the message, "I don't think the principal would approve of the recommendation you gave the teacher. You know he would want us to be honest about this." In this instance, the assistant principal hadn't talked it over with the principal, but she knew definitely what his view of the situation would be. When used judiciously, lending that authority can be effective. But the principal and assistant principal should be clear with each other about what those instances might be.

In summary, whether it is direct communication with the principal or effectively communicating with other stakeholders, many of the best practices are new ones for the assistant principal. In a broad sense, there is no substitute for active listening and precise expression, be it oral or written. But this is only a starting point. Effective administrators recognize and practice numerous other related skills that they must possess to be effective communicators.

9

Building the
Administrative Team

Strong professional relationships don't just happen; they're the product of deliberate attention.

The professional dynamic between an assistant principal and his or her other assistant principal or administrative colleagues is arguably the most important one the assistant principal has, besides the relationship with the principal. In an ideal school, these are your peers, who do the same job alongside you, the coworkers who share their good ideas and best practices with you and have your back. These are your next-door neighbors who pull you aside and keep you from "stepping in it" or saying the wrong thing at an inopportune time. In the best of situations, these are the trusted peers who want to see you succeed, grow professionally, and take appropriate risks for a simple reason: they realize that your success contributes to a stronger administrative team, better school leadership, and a more effective, well-run school.

Two Powerful Building Blocks

Administrative teams that are firing on all cylinders rarely just happen. They are usually the product of each member of the team working together to build two dynamics: loyalty and trust. Loyalty means many different things to different people, but for the administrative team, it means loyalty to the school organization and loyalty to each other. The building blocks for strong teams begin when it's evident that all of the members have a strong commitment to the school and its students.

One new assistant principal found it "hokey" when he heard his administrative colleagues continually express what effect their decisions would have on the school's reputation or whether decisions would contribute to a positive climate in the school. What he came to realize was that this was a continuation of a mindset put in place when the school first opened, when fostering a positive climate was everything. It was not artificial, but a genuine source of pride for the administrative team that they were committed in an abstract sense to the general well-being of the school for the sake of its students. The new assistant principal later admitted that the result was a stronger commitment to his day-to-day work because he saw through his fellow assistant principal's actions that this really mattered.

Trust, the other essential component, is equally as difficult to quantify. Trust is one of those "I can't describe it, but I'll know it when I see it" type of factors. As with leadership, it is sometimes easier to describe its absence than its presence. The most important factors in building trust in an administrative team are consistency and honesty.

When two new members were added to an administrative team, they made a conscious decision to run all of their potential disciplinary consequences by one another. Although time-consuming, it allowed them to process each situation, consider the salient facts, the precedent of previously incidents and their consequences, and the rationale behind each decision. By the end of the year, one assistant principal said the value was "I could almost read their minds about how they would handle a situation. We had processed enough situations together that we were arriving at the same sound conclusions." When the assistant principal took a day of leave, he didn't worry that his students would receive unreasonable consequences from another assistant principal as there was consistency and trust among them.

Honesty is a key component of trust. One assistant principal thought that he had come to a positive point in his relationship with an assistant principal colleague when she was willing to close the door and admit "I screwed up and I really need your help." Another assistant principal described honesty as being able to critique her assistant principal colleague's decisions and work and know he knows in his heart that she is saying these things for his own well being and growth. Neither of these things is easy.

Assistant Principal Assignments: The Great Balancing Act

While having assistant principals actively work together to build trust and loyalty, the principal must sometimes play the role of the great equalizer and arbiter. Often the issue that can most quickly chip away at administrative esprit de corps is assistant principal assignments and relative balance of work. A very productive practice is for the assistant principals and principal to sit down at the conclusion of each school year and revisit assistant principal assignments and responsibilities. In schools where there are multiple assistant principals, the assistant principals often follow a caseload of students at a grade level and some tasks should naturally change from year to year.

For example, the assistant principal who supervises seniors probably needs to work on graduation protocols as well as with guidance counselors to ensure that all students meet their graduation requirements. The assistant principal, who coordinates and monitors SAT/ACT tests, should probably be the administrator who supervises either juniors or seniors. Ninth grade administrators generally have the most parent meetings to attend as students adjust to high school, so this should be taken into account. A further issue is dividing the number of teachers to observe and evaluate equitably among the administrative team. Depending on the district norms, these can be extremely time-consuming processes and it is important to not overload any one assistant principal.

In one school, as per the district norm, teachers were observed each year but needed lengthy written evaluations every third year. With the supervision of specific departments, one assistant principal had 27 evaluations to write whereas a second assistant principal had five and a third assistant principal had seven to write. In this high-functioning team, the assistant principals discussed a proposal to bring to the principal to distribute the tasks more equitably so that one assistant principal wasn't so overloaded with teacher evaluations that he or she had little time for other administrative tasks. Ultimately, all members of this team were more productive as equitable sharing of duties made for a more collegial and positive working environment.

When there is constant communication, decisions aren't made in a vacuum and there is consistency and growth among all team members. Students, parents, and staff benefit because people know what to expect and the administrative team is on the same page on all issues.

Hey! I'm Doing All the Heavy Lifting Here!

It is not uncommon for an assistant principal to look around and feel like they have the heaviest workload among the members of the administrative team. This may be absolutely accurate in some cases, but in other cases, it's just perception. Some assistant principals, especially veterans who are comfortable in their role, can make the job look far easier than it actually is. In addition, it can be difficult for a new member of an administrative team who wants to fit in and feel as if they are pulling their weight among their new colleagues. Sometimes it's more realistic for a brand-new assistant principal to have less responsibility until they learn protocols, develop a routine, and figure out their strengths and challenges in their new role.

Communication is absolutely essential for an effective team to function. Each member needs to understand that fair isn't always equal and that a great deal of thought must go into determining each assistant principal's assignment. In some cases, the assistant principal may find himself in a situation where there is significant competition among the members of the administrative team. Instead of assistant principals working cooperatively they are competing with each other, creating a negative dynamic. Although some competition can be healthy among administrative team members, at an unhealthy extreme it can severely undermine the effectiveness of the entire team and, ultimately, the school. The principal must make sure that tasks and responsibilities are distributed fairly and that each assistant principal has the opportunity to grow professionally. But just as with siblings, even if all things are equal, there can be jealousy. Constant communication and validating is important from the principal. But even if everything appears to be working, some assistant principals are going to compete with each other, which can be disastrous. Strong personalities, marking territory, or people who dislike each other make for a toxic working environment that benefits nobody.

In one situation, an eager but somewhat self-centered assistant principal decided to do whatever it took to impress the principal. After report cards went out, he sent personal letters to all of the students he supervised who earned straight As. This was a nice gesture and had not been done before at the school. The assistant principal got positive feedback and felt great about it. However, he supervised grades 9 and 11 and the other assistant principal supervised grades 10 and 12. Because he didn't share his plan with the other assistant principal, she did not do the same thing. The difficulty occurred when the principal got calls from parents with students in both grades 9 and 12 in which both had straight As, but only the student in grade 9 got a letter. By not collaborating, the assistant principal ended up making the school look foolish. He had a great idea, which had he shared, would have worked to everyone's advantage and been a very positive thing.

On a highly effective team, experienced assistant principals make a point of sharing ideas and strategies with less-experienced assistant principals. Most experienced assistant principals will also admit that nothing cemented a relationship faster with a new colleague than giving them a sense of the "institutional memory" of the school, the political landscape of the key players in the community, and just simple ways to do their job more effectively in that specific school. Conversely, sometimes the new assistant principal, or one with experience in another school, may bring a wealth of new ideas and initiatives that will benefit everyone. At times when principals are faced with the decision of promoting a teacher to an assistant principal position from within or outside of the school, they will opt for the latter. This is because the outside candidate represents an opportunity for fresh approaches and avoids the "we've always done it this way" mentality among an administrative team.

Competition Is Not Always a Healthy Thing

If an assistant principal finds himself in a competitive situation with a colleague it can be uncomfortable and lead to loss of trust. In a perfect world, a closed door, sit-down, frank and honest conversation could clear the air, but often this is not the case. Members of an administrative team absolutely need each other and will always be more effective when working together. This is most clear when one assistant principal is overwhelmed and the others offer to jump in to assist. An example is when a fight occurs in the school involving numerous students who are all in the same grade and supervised by one assistant principal. In an effective team, the other assistant principals jump in with "What can I do to help?" and there is a divide-and-conquer mentality to get things sorted out and get the issue resolved appropriately and in a timely fashion. In an ineffective team, fraught with competition, either the assistant principal with ownership of the students won't distribute the students to sort through the issues or the other assistant principals don't offer to help. Worse yet, they are unwilling or refuse to assist unless directed specifically by the principal to do so.

When supervising any team, the principal must deal with distinct personalities and work through situations to solve problems. Often the principal is in the best position to observe the ebb and flow of activity among the team and can constructively prompt one assistant principal with, "Hey, your neighbor is overwhelmed with putting together the testing schedule. It might relieve some of her anxiety if you offer to cover her cafeteria duty today." At times principals need to examine their own behavior as it is possible that they are contributing to the competition. They may offer frequent praise to one assistant principal, which creates resentment and hostility in another. Worse yet is a principal who actually sets up this kind of competitive environment in the hopes of getting more work out of their assistant principals. This will be short-lived, however, because ineffective teams either explode or simmer, and in either case, they are ultimately counterproductive.

In an even worse-case scenario, the principal may be in competition with the other members of the administrative team. Specifically, this can happen with a new principal when a sitting assistant principal interviewed and didn't get the principalship. This clearly is not a good situation for anyone and all members of the team will feel the tension.

And When All Else Fails...

In some situations, regardless of what is tried the team dynamics are so poor that they are not able to be resolved. Strategies that often work to break down the barriers and improve working relationships include face-to-face meetings, honest attempts to clear the air, working with an outside mediator, an off-site retreat, or even a lunch out of the building. Unfortunately, occasionally there comes a time when one or more members of the team need to leave if there is ever to be productivity and peace. Sometimes this happens naturally through attrition but in other cases there needs to be a conscious decision for one party to move on if the team—and ultimately the school— are to function in a healthy and productive manner.

Building a cohesive, high-functioning administrative team is not easy for either the team members or the principal. Trust and loyalty are not created overnight, yet they are the essential glue that binds good teams together.

Taken a step further, rather than functioning as a collection of competent individuals, sometimes it pays for teams to adhere to the old adage, "We're only as strong as our weakest link." One veteran assistant principal expressed it this way: "It's not good enough for me to be an effective assistant principal. I need to have a stake in my coworkers being effective as well. Or as the catch phrase from an old commercial goes, 'if you don't look good, we don't look good.'"

10

Fostering Other Productive Relationships

Sometimes it's best to say, "I'd like to phone a friend, please."

Choosing Your Professional Friends Wisely

The principal–assistant principal relationship is critical to the effective development of the assistant principal, but there are other mentoring and collegial relationships that are also important. Because the principal ultimately evaluates the assistant principal, a strong working relationship with other administrative colleagues can be extremely important in the assistant principal's professional growth and development.

When a new assistant principal joins an existing administrative team, she has a steep learning curve to effectively understand and learn the culture of the team. The assistant principal needs to figure out how to best adapt and find her own niche. With some teams, this is easily done. The veteran assistant principal takes the "newbie" under his wing and works to smooth the transition by sharing information and being as helpful as possible. Unfortunately, things don't always go this smoothly. At its worst, the other assistant principals are wary of their new colleague, keep her isolated from important conversations and information, and, in doing so, create mistrust. The principal has an important role in setting expectations for the team but there is never a guarantee that everyone will play nicely in the sandbox.

Very few people rise through the ranks and become an assistant principal without help, mentoring, and guidance from someone who saw their potential and was looking out for their best interests. Often this process begins when a principal notices a teacher who always seems to go above and beyond; someone innovative, creative, and fully invested in students. Informal observations and conversations can begin to pave the way for a career in administration. One teacher had dismissed the administrative route early in her career. But her principal saw her potential and began to give her specific examples of how the successful approach she took as the Student Government Advisor was the same strategy that effective administrators use. He encouraged her to take a graduate-level course in educational administration to see if it seemed like a good fit for her skills. When she became immersed in the process, he proceeded to help her develop a 5-year career plan. This mentor became a partner in developing the teacher into a highly effective assistant principal.

Some people are fortunate and have a true visionary as a mentor, someone who can help them craft a plan to reach their goal to become an assistant principal. This may mean a long-range plan that includes coursework for certification, committees, and other experiences that develop a viable candidate for an assistant principal position. When this happens, often that person assumes a guiding and mentoring role for a long time in the assistant principal's tenure. But most people can point to multiple forces and people who contributed to their professional development along the way.

Who Is On Your Speed Dial?

The best professional relationships in administration often have nothing to do with career paths, mentoring, and long-term plans. Sometimes the very best resource an assistant principal can have is a trusted peer on the other end of the phone, who shares similar challenges but is at a different location. This is a person who understands the assistant principal role and is able to provide a fresh perspective, a creative new solution or basic guidance. Often they are an assistant principal in another location, or someone who served as an assistant principal at some point in their career.

One seasoned principal said that people's ranking on his speed-dial spoke volumes about their importance to him. His spouse was #1, closely followed by his assistant principal peer. This was the person he could call and laugh with and share, without judgment, all of the ridiculous things that happen on any given day in his life as an assistant principal. These assistant principals had a sibling assistant principal relationship as they started their careers on the same administrative team. They were trained in a similar way, had similar experiences, and shared similar philosophies. When one assistant principal moved to another school, the relationship was cemented as an integral part of their experiences, if for nothing else the inside jokes and ability to laugh at each other and themselves.

These peers were fortunate to have parallel careers, serving 1 year as assistant principals in the same school, followed by several years as assistant principals in other schools, as middle school principals, and eventually as high school principals. Having the bond of that special peer relationship made reality checks a daily occurrence and ultimately made both better administrators. At the end of the day, one would call the other and without even saying hello would begin with, "You won't believe what happened today...." This healthy exchange often resulted in hysterical laughter and created a sense of balance for both of them.

Often one would call the other and say, "This is what I am thinking of doing, tell me if I am about to do something really stupid." (Which, of course, shows they had the good sense to call before they actually did it and got into hot water.) Perhaps the healthiest part of the relationship was that neither carried the burden home of what happened that day as they were able to process and gain a better perspective by discussing it. Both were convinced that being able to vent at work allowed them to spare their spouses the worst part of their days and have more balanced professional and personal lives.

The Value of the Cohort: Mix and Match Your Own

Resourceful assistant principals will find a trusted peer and communicate frequently with that peer. The point is not to rehash every event, but to gain a healthy perspective and a reality check that may not be available in the daily grind of doing the job. Sometimes someone at another location, who doesn't know the players, can offer an objective opinion and a fresh perspective on a situation. Often this same person can ask the tough questions that make it easier to come up with reasonable solutions. Someone on the outside looking in is often better able to see the big picture when the person enmeshed in it can't see the forest for the trees. This is the colleague who has a vested interest in seeing you succeed and won't flatter you with half-truths. Trust and honesty, without ego are the key factors in this successful relationship.

In some districts with a formalized assistant principal training program, there is a cohort of assistant principals who are trained together and share many bonding experiences. In large districts, this group may be as large as 12 to 15 assistant principals training at the same time, which is a wonderful opportunity for networking and developing career-long friendships and relationships. In other districts, a single assistant principal is fortunate if they have one new peer coming into the position when they do. The difficulty is keeping any group, regardless of size, from becoming competitive as eventually this is the same group that potentially could be interviewing against each other for principal opportunities. When a cohort works best, assistant principals rely on each other for support and advice as each will have a very different experience, depending on which school they work in and which principal they work for. This network of peers at similar places in their career can be an extremely valuable resource.

One group of six assistant principals chose to continue their relationship after their training experience was over. They met monthly at one of the assistant principal's homes and rotated who brought snacks and wine. This became a sacred ritual, in a safe environment where they could share and learn from each other in a highly collegial way. They chose not to meet in a restaurant as they recognized the possibility of being overheard and confidentiality was the key to this group relationship being productive. Although it could have become a monthly gripe session, it instead became a positive and healthy way to share and problem solve. The power of this group continued when some of the members became principals as they knew they had trusted friends to depend on for advice and support.

In a different situation, another assistant principal worked in a medium-size district, but didn't have the luxury of a formalized peer cohort. Through years of attendance at central office meetings, required trainings, and external professional conferences she had come to know a group she referred to as her "Fabulous Five." Each had a different area of expertise, professional strength, or superpower in the eyes of this colleague. If the assistant principal had a difficult parent concern, she called Fabulous Five #1, who was a master with parents. If the problem was a staff issue, she called Fabulous Five #2 who worked in the school system's human relations department and usually had the answer. When complex data challenges, Fabulous Five #3 was "the man." Each was valuable in providing a different perspective and, they would often recommend calling another one of the Fabulous Five for another perspective. Only two had ever worked together in the same school, but out of necessity they formed this healthy professional relationship. The assistant principal who dubbed them the Fabulous Five was someone who functioned best with others as a sounding board. Sometimes her assistant principal colleague in the next office was the perfect person, but in other instances her gut told her to pick up the phone for one of her Fabulous Five "specialists."

The Person Who Really Runs the School

Many new assistant principals are fortunate to have secretarial or administrative support at their disposal. Yet, this may be the first time when they've had this resource available to them. The challenge is learning how to delegate appropriately and how to use secretarial support effectively. As classroom teachers, educators are accustomed to being self-sufficient. Most teachers write their own teaching materials or work with colleagues to develop tests, graphic organizers, handouts, outlines, etc. In some schools there is copying assistance, but in most, teachers do much of their own clerical work. So when a teacher transitions into the role of the assistant principal, they often need to figure out what and how to delegate appropriately to others.

A highly effective and skilled secretary can make the assistant principal's job far easier. When either is new to their position, it makes sense to sit down and talk about reasonable expectations and how they can work effectively, with mutual respect, as a team. Secretaries and administrative assistants are amazing at multitasking but they also need timelines and clear communication. One assistant principal found the secretary he worked with to be an outstanding writer and editor. He found he could rough out what he needed written and she could give him back a draft to work with. In other cases, he would give her a document and ask her to clean it up for him and put it on letterhead. For routine items, this became a timesaver for both as they evolved into an effective team.

Administrative assistants may be used to keep the administrator's calendar once a good working relationship is established. Many assistant principals find it hard to relinquish that control but also find it saves them a great deal of time scheduling appointments and meetings when their assistant takes over that task.

The flip side of the assistant principal–administrative assistant relationship is when too much is delegated to the administrative assistant. Assistant principals need to be careful to keep a reasonable check and balance in that relationship as no one, particularly someone in a subordinate position, should feel dumped on.

Looking for Friends in All the Right Places

Some assistant principals are fortunate enough to have "friends in high places." This can be a mixed blessing and it is very important not to abuse this relationship. It can be very tempting when the assistant principal has a friend who can help him when things aren't going well. The reality is he would be better served in the long run by going through channels and handling things as though the friend wasn't a factor. An assistant principal should never go behind the principal's back, unless something is so egregious that it would be negligent to ignore. But having a friend in high places can be a tremendous asset to the assistant principal as long as the relationship is not abused.

One assistant principal had a close relationship with an associate superintendent through his involvement with his church. The associate superintendent served as a father figure and helped guide the assistant principal appropriately. The assistant principal understood that conversations about what was happening at school needed to be neutral. When he needed guidance or advice, he was very careful to keep it appropriate. This assistant principal understood the fine line between consulting the associate superintendent for advice and tattling on the principal.

Some assistant principals are fortunate enough to have a retired colleague as a mentor. In this case, the wisdom of someone who has seen it all and done it all can be extremely helpful to the assistant principal. The mentor can be an objective listener, often with infinite wisdom. Other assistant principals, particularly those in small districts where collaboration with other assistant principals is difficult, can benefit from online discussions through professional organization listserves. As long as too much identifying information isn't shared about specific situations, this can be a valuable resource. Assistant principals who are fortunate enough to attend professional conferences have the opportunity to meet assistant principals in different districts or parts of the country. This networking and potential benchmarking relationship is extremely valuable as it can help assistant principals feel less isolated and also help guide them through some of the more universal issues common to assistant principals.

One assistant principal maintained his most trusted friend was a person who knew little about the world of high school, but knew a great deal about him—his wife. She was his most trusted source, his best reality check. Sometimes when he picked up the phone what he needed was some nonjudgmental "required listening time" on the other end. Other times, he needed her to cut through the politics and minutia of "educationese" and remind him what his core values were. But most times, he just needed a little reassurance from her that "it would all work out" and something to make him laugh.

Regardless of how it is accomplished, having a trusted and objective friend/mentor or ally on the other end of the phone or an e-mail can make all the difference in the assistant principal's development and ultimate success.

11

Help! I'm a Brand-New Assistant Principal and I'm Drowning!

What to do when you find yourself as a rookie in the deep end of the administrative pool.

The New Assistant Principal: Bring Your Life Vest

Even the most competent new assistant principals often feel like fish out of water Their familiar teacher routines are gone, they are working with a new team of professionals, and they are often left to problem solve many challenges on their own. There are numerous pitfalls for new assistant principals to avoid and sometimes success is defined by the novice as "not having failed."

Induction for a new assistant principal is similar to that of a new teacher, but without the benefit of a student-teaching experience or practicum. Some districts have extensive training programs that are multitiered with consultants, monthly meetings, training around a variety of relevant topics, and a cohort group of assistant principal colleagues at the same level of experience. Yet this huge investment of time, manpower, and money does not automatically guarantee a successful assistant principal experience. At the other extreme are districts where the assistant principal is thrown into the position, left to sink or swim with little guidance or support, much like many brand-new teachers facing a classroom full of students for the very first time. The majority of assistant principals, however, probably find themselves somewhere between those two extremes.

People apply (or are tapped) to be an assistant principal, because they have demonstrated the skills necessary to be successful administrators. Most are outstanding teachers, have a strong work ethic, demonstrate exceptional organizational skills, relate well to people, have a genuine concern for the well-being of students, have the ability to see the "big picture," and are highly respected and eager to learn. Although that should be enough to guarantee a successful career as an assistant principal, sadly, it does not. Some assistant principals are in the right place at the right time, whereas others wait patiently for many years for an assistant principal vacancy to become available. But regardless of how they got there, most assistant principals quickly learn that not all of the skills that served them well as a classroom teacher transfer to their new position.

Your Assignment: How to Avoid Drawing the Short Straw

Often the new assistant principal gets the least-desirable assignments in a school, as veteran assistant principals are thrilled to be able to pass off the tasks they dislike. These might include master scheduling or the responsibility of organizing the multitude of tests administered in schools. Although this is hardly a fair or reasonable way to determine responsibilities, it is often the way things are done. The new assistant principal may be reluctant to rock the boat or seem like she is not up to the task or a team player. This is when it makes sense to take a deep breath, assess the situation, and decide who you should listen to, who you should talk to, when and why.

It is incumbent upon principals to ensure a new assistant principal isn't assigned or doesn't take on too many responsibilities, particularly when she is learning the job or is new to the school. Even the most potentially effective assistant principal can quickly become overwhelmed when everything is new and she hasn't figured out her best resources and supports.

One assistant principal was assigned to write a new bell schedule every time there needed to be an adjustment for a new testing program. The assistant principal quickly became aware that there was a very negative group of teachers who would contact the teachers' union if they believed their contract was being infringed upon, especially when it came to work hours and planning time. Prior to putting her first bell schedule out to staff, she asked the ring leader of this group if he would mind looking it over for her to see if he saw any obvious pitfalls or problems with it. The teacher was flattered to be included in the process and gave his blessing for the schedule after suggesting some minor adjustments. The staff had no recourse but to accept the schedule and there was little grumbling. The assistant principal made a point of getting the teacher's stamp of approval on subsequent bell schedules and there were no further issues. This assistant principal turned a potentially negative teacher into an ally and resource and avoided an unnecessary power struggle.

In one large school, the principal made a conscious decision to subdivide some tasks among assistant principals that would have been taken on by one person in another school. In this case, the testing coordinator position was divided so no one assistant principal would be overwhelmed by the organizational tasks. This meant the new assistant principal could learn his testing responsibilities with backup, support, and in a manner that didn't potentially cause his other responsibilities to be dropped. One of the assistant principals took on PSAT, SAT, and ACT testing coordination and data analysis, another took the state standardized testing, and the third coordinated final and Advanced Placement exams. This plan worked for all concerned as they each had a piece of the pie with significant responsibilities and ownership. This model also meant they were able to take on some of the more interesting initiatives in the school and no one person was bogged down with one thing. The added benefit was that there was always backup and support for each aspect of the testing program, and none of the balls being juggled in the air were dropped.

Piling Your Plate Too High and Other Hazards

Usually the new assistant principal has a strong desire to demonstrate their leadership ability to their new principal and their other administrative colleagues. This all comes from a well-intended mindset: the rookie wants to be a team player and demonstrate that he is capable of doing his fair share. Like a hungry patron at a buffet, he soon begins to fill his "plate" with projects that he believes he can accomplish. He agrees to facilitate a new initiative, or take on that tough nut issue that other administrators can't seem to crack. The depth and breadth of these assignments soon begin to pile up. Because the new assistant principal really doesn't have a good frame of reference for the scope and complexity of his job, oftentimes he is overwhelmed and needs to look for ways to remove some of the various items from his plate. The solution to avoiding this problem may be to adopt a "go slow" approach until the new assistant principal can get his arms around the ebb and flow of his new role. In this instance, the principal's role is to encourage and feed initiative, but temper the assistant principal with gentle doses of reality.

In one case, a very competent assistant principal had her first interaction with a very negative parent who used racist terms in talking to her. The assistant principal repeatedly gritted her teeth when dealing with this parent and did her best to work as positively as possible with the student and parent. The student had extensive absences and when the assistant principal called the parent, the parent berated her and was verbally abusive. The assistant principal finally reached her limit and told the parent that the conversation was over. She was extremely shaken and went into the principal fighting back tears. The principal listened, commiserated, and advised the assistant principal to go for a walk or a drive to clear her head. The assistant principal left for an hour and came back ready to process what had happened and come up with a strategy on how to deal with this parent in the future. The principal was able to validate the assistant principal's concerns (and outrage) and also recognize that she needed to cool down before she could discuss something so emotional and personal. He processed with the assistant principal and allowed her to save face and move on in a more productive direction.

Lines of Communication: Keeping Them Untangled

It's important for every assistant principal to have a trusted colleague with whom she can vent, bounce ideas off of, and sometimes just obtain a reality check. Some of the most effective assistant principals are the ones who trust someone enough to call (or walk into the office next door) and say, "Well, that didn't work!" Just being able to express your failures to someone you trust, someone who doesn't evaluate you and won't judge you (and is able to laugh with you), is a huge step toward reflection and being able to learn from what did or did not work.

In one school, the three assistant principals routinely pow-wowed before bringing situations to their principal. This became a common practice as a way to process issues and to be sure they made uniform recommendations to the principal. It wasn't that they were afraid to ask the principal questions, but they found they made more informed recommendations to him when they worked things through as a team.

Effective assistant principals learn to leave their egos at the door and admit when they are completely stumped in handling something. When an assistant principal brings a problem to her principal, the response from the principal should be, "How do you want to handle it? What do you think?" As any good teacher knows, giving the student the answer doesn't really help them and creates a dependency that can inhibit their growth and learning. Being able to talk through the difficult scenarios without fear of repercussion or judgment builds on the assistant principal's previous experiences and boosts not only confidence, but professional effectiveness.

Assistant principals need to determine what to figure out for themselves, what to talk to a trusted colleague about, and when to go directly to the principal for advice, direction, or to process. That decision usually has a great deal to do with the culture of the school, the effectiveness of the administrative team, and the urgency or need for a decision. Obviously, in an emergency, it is incumbent upon the assistant principal to go directly to the principal, particularly when safety and security is involved. Most principals want to see independence in their assistant principals but they also don't ever want to be blind-sided by a significant decision the assistant principal made without alerting the principal. Those are the decisions that can come back to bite the principal and can often take on a life of their own.

The Tortoise or the Hare: Who Really Has the Advantage?

The difficulty for the assistant principal is recognizing the fine line between showing initiative and jumping the gun. Sometimes the assistant principal takes action without getting input, creates a plan, and gets multiple steps down the road on a project or issue. The reality is that most steps in any complex leadership task benefit from running it by the principal. The worst-case scenario is that once the assistant principal gets too far out on a limb or makes a poor decision, there can be retreat, backtracking, and embarrassment experienced by the assistant principal. A novice assistant principal should be asking a lot of questions and listening a great deal, particularly if she is both new to the school, figuring out the school culture, is new to the role of assistant principal, and learning the many facets of the job. Principals should expect and encourage questions and frank, fruitful discussions.

The most effective decisions are made after gathering as much input and information as possible so as to make the very best decision. The assistant principal is called upon to make many decisions throughout the day, yet often jumps to make some decisions that could (and should) be delayed. An example is that when a fight occurs in school, it most typically results in the parties involved having severe disciplinary consequences. However, there is usually a great deal of information to sort through: how did the fight start; who started it; what preceded the event; is there a history with these students; was it a first time offense; was either party injured and to what extent; what was the motive; were there any extenuating circumstances; etc. It may also include questions regarding racial overtones, drugs, weapons, gang activity, etc. On face value, a fight may look like a simple disagreement between two students when in fact it may be much more involved and have greater school and community implications.

The first phone call the assistant principal makes to parents could go one of many ways. In one scenario, the assistant principal calls the parent, tells the parent that her child was in a fight and is being suspended for ten days, and asks the parent to come pick him up. But what if one student was clearly the aggressor and one is seriously injured? Suppose the injured student started the whole mess, for example, over a drug deal? At the time of the incident, the assistant principal needs to gather as much information as possible from both the students involved in the fight and any witnesses before sending the students home. It is very appropriate to call the parent and say that the student needs to go home and stay home, but that you will call the next day with complete information regarding consequences. This allows adequate time to investigate thoroughly and discuss the matter with the principal. Assistant principals must sometimes resist the temptation to expediently bring issues to closure just to get things off their plate or appear decisive. Having time to process the event with other members of the administrative team, the principal and security personnel will ultimately make for a better decision. A decision made quickly, or when you are angry is rarely a reasonable and effective decision.

When Neatness Doesn't Count

One novice assistant principal was most interested in wrapping issues up and leaving every day with a clean desk. He became an independent contractor and sometimes made knee-jerk decisions without consulting his peers or the principal. One student issue blew up as there were nuances about the situation that the assistant principal had not considered prior to making a disciplinary decision. The principal sat him down for a frank discussion. The principal needed the assistant principal to understand that some issues are never really over and that the difficult student or parent or staff member will probably reappear with an even greater issue shortly in the future. The principal advised that if the situation was handled judiciously and with great care, it is less likely to reoccur.

In any situation in which a decision was made (be it disciplinary, academic, athletic, etc.), if more information comes to light, adjusting that decision to the benefit of the student is always appropriate. There is nothing wrong with calling a parent to say you reconsidered your decision based on additional information; in fact, it can increase the assistant principal's credibility as someone willing to do whatever it takes to be fair to students.

Taking Your Cues from Others

A new assistant principal can and should request modeling from veteran administrators in the instructional supervision of teachers. Depending on the norms of the district, an effective method is for a novice assistant principal to observe a teacher alongside a veteran assistant principal or the principal. This is best done in an announced observation of an effective teacher, with the teacher's permission to have two observers at the same time. If the assistant principal is observing with a veteran observer, there is an opportunity to compare and reflect upon what each observer saw in the class. This is an effective teachable moment for the principal and an opportunity for the assistant principal to see what the principal is focusing on in the classroom.

A new assistant principal should never be reluctant to ask for help or admit when she needs assistance. Frequently the dilemma is in knowing when to ask or even what the question is. Each unique situation brings a different set of variables: What's in the student's best interest? What is the principal's philosophy on similar issues? Where is there clarity and where is there ambiguity? In many instances, there is not a clear cut point of when to wait or when to act. Regardless, one fact remains: It can be a very lonely job if done in a vacuum. Collegial sharing, questioning, and reflecting, although requiring a certain level of trust, helps the entire administrative team function at a higher level to the benefit of students, teachers, and a safe and positive learning environment.

12

Why Try New Things If I Know What I Do Well?

The dos and don'ts of taking on new administrative assignments.

Logic Doesn't Always Make the Most Sense

It seems logical that when a school has more than one assistant principal, each should be assigned the departments and tasks that are most aligned with their previous experiences, comfort level, and areas of expertise. If an assistant principal was a math teacher, it probably makes sense that she should supervise the math department. And if she is good at math, she probably will be the master scheduler and perhaps also work with school finance. If he was a coach, he would be the perfect choice to supervise athletics. An assistant principal who was a guidance counselor would be best suited to work with student issues, but probably not discipline, as she may be too lenient. The most organized assistant principal is perfect to be the testing coordinator. In fact, the best assistant principal in a school should automatically get the heaviest load if the school is to be well run. This all make perfect sense, right?

It makes perfect sense if the objective is to burn out the assistant principals, not allow anyone to stretch and grow, and to stifle any or all creativity in the school. Furthermore, it inhibits professional growth opportunities, sustainability in a school practices and procedures, and eliminates opportunities for each assistant principal to learn all aspects of running a school—skills that are required if they aspire to be a principal. If everyone only did what was comfortable for them, then what happens if one assistant principal leaves and his responsibilities need to be redistributed? Does everything fall apart? And who bears the burden of figuring out what needs to be done and how to accomplish each task and responsibility?

Effective principals understand the balancing act of working with assistant principals in multifaceted ways and the importance of new opportunities and growth for professional development. There are a huge number of leadership responsibilities and management tasks that must be accomplished in any school and the principal needs to be a key stakeholder in determining how tasks are delegated. A great deal of thought needs to be put into why a particular assistant principal has a specific administrative assignment and how that may change from year to year. In some schools, "this is the way we've always done it" may appear to work, but not if there is an eye toward mentoring and development for the assistant principals.

Stepping Outside Your Comfort Zone Without "Stepping in It"

Each assistant principal is most effective when he or she is not on automatic pilot. A little professional discomfort can be a good thing, particularly if it causes you to look at things through a different lens and step outside of your comfort zone. If the same assistant principal has always been the testing coordinator, chances are the testing runs like a well-oiled machine. Or does it? Perhaps when someone new looks at it, they see a logical but different way of approaching the tasks at hand. There is a fine line between "if it ain't broke, don't fix it" and tweaking something to end up with a better product. But one of the trickier things to navigate in this situation is the give and take between the assistant principal who previously had the assignment and the assistant principal new to the assignment.

A good example is the coordination of the graduation ceremony. Schools tend to set a pattern and stick with what they have always done and what works best for them. However, an assistant principal doing some research and exploring how other schools approach student speakers, the order of events, etc., can bring positive changes that improve an already effective process. Or flaws in the graduation process may become apparent, necessitating a change, and hopefully resulting in a more smoothly run and effective ceremony. One assistant principal, who worked in several different schools as a teacher, was able to provide his school with a wealth of knowledge about how graduations differed between several schools. Through a great deal of discussion, the administrative team was able to work with the class sponsor and students to use these new ideas to make some significant upgrades to the graduation process. But the process was improved because the administrators and other school personnel were open to the possibility of change. Schools that are steeped in tradition can miss valuable opportunities for improvement by not shaking things up from time to time and encouraging assistant principals to explore new options and ideas.

When you are an assistant principal taking on a new assignment that puts you outside of your comfort zone, there are a number of general rules of thumb that apply. First, be a quick study and digest as much information quickly about the new task. If it's creating a smaller learning community within a school, read the literature, do a site visit, and talk to as many experts as you can in a short time. Get a complete sense of the issue. Second, talk with the people who previously had ownership of the leadership area. What works? What doesn't? What changes would they propose? Next, in putting your own stamp on the leadership area or task, avoid the extremes. Rarely is it the case that every decision associated with the previous regime was wrong and needs changing.

One assistant principal found himself in charge of the school field trip approval process. There was a complicated two-page form that teachers had to complete to get their field trips scheduled. Many staff members complained that it served as a disincentive for teachers who might otherwise run field trips. The assistant principal decided that the form could easily be simplified, and single-handedly made some significant changes, omitting large sections of the previous form. Because he failed to discuss the form with stakeholders, what he didn't realize was that each part of the form had a specific, important purpose that had evolved over several years. In simplifying the process, he had cut several key personnel out of the knowledge loop and, worse yet, was in violation of district policy. Although it appeared that he made the teaching staff happy, he actually created a real mess. Doing it differently can involve subtle changes that produce profoundly different and better results. There should be a natural inclination when taking on a new task to build on what was previously done, and involve those who have a broad understanding in the process. For the assistant principal who is taking the risk of trying new things, understanding the fine line between going too slowly and making changes that are too sweeping or done too quickly is often the trickiest part of the balancing act.

Venturing WAY Out of Your Comfort Zone

So what happens when the administrator who was a former music teacher is assigned to supervise the English department? Does supervision and instruction deteriorate and student achievement drop? Or does the assistant principal's knowledge of effective instructional practices transfer to a different subject matter? If it doesn't, it's a red flag and a clear indication to the principal that the assistant principal needs more training on instructional practices.

A perfect example is when an assistant principal who doesn't speak a word of Spanish observes an upper-level Spanish class, where the entire class is conducted in Spanish. The challenge for the assistant principal is getting beyond the language barrier to the strategies the teacher is using: who is called on, student responses, body language, transition between activities, nonverbal responses, and how much the assistant principal is able to actually understand in the lesson without understanding a single spoken word. On many levels, this can build the assistant principal's capacity and confidence in her knowledge of instruction. Most good supervision of instruction is less about the specific curriculum and more about teaching and learning.

The assistant principal needs to understand that a well-run art classroom, physical education class, or a science lab, where there is movement and conversation, looks very different from a structured class where students sit in rows and raise their hands throughout the lesson. They also need to recognize that just because a classroom appears to be highly structured it actually could mean that little learning is occurring. If an assistant principal can successfully differentiate, observe, and supervise subjects out of her comfort zone (in some cases way out of her comfort zone), then she is far better equipped to deal with all disciplines across the curriculum and to increase her proficiency as an instructional leader. Likewise, when an assistant principal has conferences with members of a department whose subject matter is unfamiliar to her, and consistently provides these teachers with meaningful feedback, the assistant principal builds all-important confidence in her skills as an instructional leader, regardless of the subject.

Again, the principal needs to work with the assistant principal to strike a balance between the familiar and unfamiliar in the assistant principal position. If *every* assignment in the administrative portfolio represents a new challenge for the assistant principal, chances are the assistant principal will be too overwhelmed to be effective. If possible, a brand-new assistant principal *should* be assigned to supervise the departments the assistant principal is most comfortable with, as all the other tasks and most aspects of the job will be new to her. What should never happen is to completely overwhelm an assistant principal (particularly someone new to the school and new to the job) with so many new things that she struggles and possibly fails. If a new assistant principal is hired to "fill an existing slot" rather than to have her strengths and areas of opportunity be best matched up with her skills, the assistant principal's chances of being successful are greatly diminished.

A new assistant principal was hired to replace an eight-year veteran who moved on to a principalship. The new assistant principal had many of the strengths, at least on paper, that the previous assistant principal possessed. Both had backgrounds as strong special education teachers; both had demonstrated outstanding organizational skills; both had outgoing, student-centered personalities; and both had an excellent rapport with students and parents. So the new assistant principal was assigned to supervise the special education department plus two other departments, testing coordination (which included a brand-new high-stakes state assessment), the master schedule, planning for graduation, and a caseload of 450 students. There was virtually no support or guidance offered by either the principal or the other assistant principals in the school. This was truly a sink-or-swim situation. By the end of the first semester, the principal evaluated the new assistant principal out of his position. He was so overwhelmed by the huge responsibilities he assumed, that his confidence quickly eroded and he felt paralyzed. Perhaps the new assistant principal wasn't as good a candidate as the principal originally thought, but it is highly possible that the overload of new things and the huge responsibilities assumed from the veteran assistant principal were just too overwhelming for a novice who was fresh out of the classroom going into an assistant principal position. Had the new assistant principal been assigned special education, two additional departments, a student grade level, and some managerial tasks not as monumental as graduation, standardized testing, and the master schedule, perhaps he would have been a successful assistant principal and with time, grown in the position and been able to handle all of the tasks, as had his predecessor.

It Isn't the "What" of New Things, It's the "Who"

The more one examines how to best try new things the more one will find that success is less dictated by the skill set or the previous experience of the administrator new to the task. It is much more important for the administrator to be willing to reach out to the other stakeholders, seek guidance, collaborate, and learn all of the interpersonal aspects of the situation. One assistant principal thought that "My most important resource in leading was always the person in the office next to me—a sounding board, the veteran with the school's institutional memory, the creative 'brainstormer.'" When stability and trust exists on an administrative team, most of its members learn from each other, and there is very little that assistant principals cannot learn, lead or manage, when they have enthusiastic collaborators one or two doors away.

But when change comes to administrative teams, and new members replace loyal colleagues, trying new things is not always by choice, but represents a decision made or brought on by others. Sometimes a situation arises when a new principal comes in with an eye on changing existing procedures. Some principals are brought in specifically to be change agents. The veteran assistant principal or administrative team can be the guardian of the status quo or can use this change as an opportunity to process with the principal what has been done in the past and why, with the recognition that they need to be open to changes and adjustments. One assistant principal resented the fact that her new principal was insisting that she look at student results from a data-oriented perspective. The previous principal, a beloved figure in the community, had taken a more "what does your gut tell you" approach to student achievement, which, over time, had begun to serve the students in the school less and less. The most significant hurdle the assistant principal had to get over was the mindset that the new principal was not evil for wanting to change the comfortable ways of the past. The combination of new ideas and existing traditions and procedures, if handled well by all members of an administrative team, can result in significant school improvement.

Developing an Interchangeable Team

In a school where the assistant principal's tasks and assignments are determined and set in stone, it behooves the assistant principal to discuss with the principal and other assistant principals some movement so as to keep everyone from getting stale. Sometimes adjusting who supervises one department or task can open doors for the entire administrative team and allow for creativity and growth. As leadership opportunities are traded and reshuffled among members of administrative teams, it is equally as important to trade off the organizational plans, the effective memo, and other tried-and-true best practices. Nothing builds trust faster between a new and veteran assistant principal as when the veteran says, "I know you're in charge of the annual arts assembly this year. Here's my folder from last year. Feel free to use what you like and discard what you think doesn't work. And please talk to me about it if you want some help." In highly effective administrative teams, assistant principals mentor other members of the team in the management of tasks so that the base of areas of expertise is broadened. This also means that if something happens and an assistant principal leaves, or even is ill on the day of a particular event she had planned, a fellow assistant principal can step in and take over. The other benefits of this "pay it forward" method are also obvious: The veteran assistant principal strengthens her own skills by assisting in the mentoring of a novice assistant principal or a colleague who is taking on a new responsibility. It compels the veteran assistant principal to process why she does the things she does the way she does out loud. This metacognition strengthens the whole framework for leadership. It helps assistant principals build their resume for other career opportunities down the line. Perhaps most importantly, it cements the professional and personal bonds among the administrative team as they venture to try new things together.

13

When a Crisis Hits (and It Will)

Some say "crisis planning" is a contradiction in terms; but are there lessons to be learned?

It is inevitable that every assistant principal will be involved in or charged with managing a crisis situation sometime in his or her tenure. Crises can come in many forms and no matter how many emergency plans are on file, every crisis has its own personality and there can be unforeseen circumstances and events. Although the assistant principal would like the comfort of having the principal at school to take command of the situation, often things happen when the principal is away from the building, or a crisis is so large that each member of the administrative team must take on a unique leadership role. The operational word is *team*, as the functioning of the administrative team is the key component in effective crisis management.

The Lessons of 9/11

September 11, 2001, taught school-based administrators what crisis management is about. Schools in the New York and Washington, DC, areas had a unique burden, but the great unknown weighed on every school administrator in the United States. In effective teams, the assistant principals and principal grouped immediately for a rapid division of labors. Each member had his or her own distinctive perspective and could bring something to the table.

In one school, the assistant principals quickly fell into their natural and respective roles. The assistant principal who was known to work most effectively with the nuts and bolts of running the school immediately pulled out the school map and divided the school into zones for security purposes. (Remember that this was before most districts had complex crisis plans.) The logistics-prone assistant principal called for all available personnel and delegated assignments. The practical assistant principal grabbed a bull horn and went to the outside of the building to direct traffic issues caused by parents arriving in a panic to pick up their children. The more nurturing assistant principal went immediately to the front lines to calm frantic parents and teachers.

The actions of the administrative team allowed the principal to make more global and big-picture decisions and communicate regularly with district-level staff, teachers, and other school staff to keep everyone—especially students—informed and, most importantly, calm and safe. In this case, each assistant principal naturally did what they did best and complemented each other's strengths while meeting the safety and security needs of the school population. There was no sense of panic, but rather a coming together of the entire school community and a spirit that they would all get through this together, no matter what. The cohesiveness of this team laid the groundwork for how they handled future situations as they learned quickly they could trust and depend on each other through the most stressful of times.

In contrast, at a neighboring school, where the administrative team did not communicate or work well together, there was little or no information provided to students and staff, resulting in widespread panic and, ultimately, chaos. This school administrative staff had a great deal of team-building work to do to build trust and a professional relationship that would prevent this kind of reaction from occurring again in future emergency situations.

The Most Important Resource in a Crisis: Quick Thinking and Common Sense

Each assistant principal needs to know who they are in a crisis. Although we sometimes don't have the luxury of choosing our role, adrenaline is an amazing thing. Even the most squeamish of people can deal with blood when there isn't a choice. But if you know that you are better at crowd control than at comforting someone who is seriously injured, and there is someone willing and able to be the comforter, then managing crowd control is where you should be, as this is how the students and school are best served.

One of the most critical things an assistant principal must do is assess a situation quickly and determine whether or not there is imminent danger and if there is, just what that means. There are many heroic actions that can occur, but the assistant principal needs to understand the line between keeping students' safe and putting themselves in harm's way. Sometimes holding back to manage a situation is the most courageous thing an assistant principal can do, as it will have an impact on the safety of a larger group.

In one case, an assistant principal was serving as summer school principal at a neighboring school. At the end of the session, when students were dismissed, a fight broke out among some students and some gang-involved adult intruders. In a split second what could have been an easily resolved scuffle, turned into a stabbing incident with serious injuries to the victim. The assistant principal was called upon to deal with this horrible situation with traumatized students, heavy police involvement, the media, and eventually huge community issues. Nothing in this assistant principal's experience prepared him for such a horrific event, yet he handled all aspects of it perfectly, based on his own character, judgment, life experiences, calling on appropriate resources, and the knowledge he gained dealing with smaller, difficult situations in his training as an assistant principal.

Sometimes a situation that seems like a regular discipline event to an assistant principal can escalate into something far more dramatic. A novice female assistant principal questioned a male student who was a suspected drug dealer. She kept the student talking while, unbeknownst to the student, the police were on their way to interrogate and probably arrest him. There was a multifaceted situation going on, involving the principal and another assistant principal, so this assistant principal was on her own. The student insisted he needed to go to the restroom; the assistant principal recognized that if he had drugs on him, this would be his opportunity to dispose of them. So the assistant principal continued to engage the student in conversation as a stall technique. Although in this case, the tactic worked, the assistant principal foolishly put herself in a dangerous situation with a potentially violent student. When the student was arrested, he not only was in possession of illegal drugs, he also had a weapon. Had the assistant principal not established a rapport with this student, the end result could have been tragic injury to her. It was a foolish and irresponsible risk on the part of the assistant principal, even if in this case the end result was a positive one.

When the Principal's Away…

In some crisis situations there is police involvement and they take charge of the situation, but in most cases, the principal is the crisis commander. When the principal is out of the building and the assistant principal is in charge, the assistant principal needs to be completely familiar with the nuances of the school building and be intimately knowledgeable about all of the protocols in the school emergency plan. The assistant principal needs to know who the key players are on the staff that can be counted on in an emergency, and most importantly, needs to be willing to step up and make the difficult decisions, often without a great deal of time to think things through and process all possibilities. When a bomb threat has been phoned in and it's freezing cold outside, factors need to be weighed as to the magnitude of the threat, whether or not the school is to be evacuated, and what provisions will be made for students—all within a very short time frame. This is a huge responsibility but every assistant principal must face the possibility that when they become an assistant principal, this is potentially part of the job. The process assistant principals use to make decisions in times of crisis are often a reflection of their previous experiences and training in crisis management, even when they may seem to be low-level threats.

One assistant principal found herself in charge when both the principal and the more veteran assistant principal, who was usually in charge in the principal's absence, were both out of the building at an administrative meeting. Mid morning, the security team leader informed her that he had just been contacted by his supervisor at the district level that the school needed to go into a lockdown situation as there was a burglary in progress in the immediate neighborhood. The police had reported that the suspect was confronted by the homeowner, panicked, and ran. The suspect appeared to be of high school age, and although not necessarily a student in the school, might try to enter and attempt to blend in with the student body. The assistant principal was well-trained and remained calm. She gathered the emergency response team, briefed them, and called the code for a lockdown. Once that was done, she e-mailed the principal that the code had been implemented.

The team monitored the building according to protocol. Doors were locked and monitored, instruction continued, and halls were kept clear. A plan was developed as to how to deal with lunch and a modified plan was quickly developed. After approximately a half hour, a call came in from the police that the suspect had been apprehended. The emergency code was lifted, the assistant principal made an announcement, and the regular school day resumed. However, that was not the full story.

As all of this was occurring, the principal was pulled out of the meeting by her supervisor and asked what was going on in her school. The local radio station was receiving calls asking what was happening as apparently students were texting and calling their parents and parents were calling the radio station looking for accurate information. Because she was not able to monitor her e-mail during the meeting and no one had called her, the principal had no idea what was going on. When she contacted the assistant principal, and learned what was happening, she asked the assistant principal many questions: Had she called the supervisory office to alert them to the situation? Did she call the PTA president? Did she use the phone messaging system to give parents an update? None of these things had happened during the management of the crisis situation.

The assistant principal was able to quickly rectify these oversights and no harm was done. The assistant principal's basic instincts were good and she kept students and staff safe throughout the situation and she got a great deal of positive feedback. She remained calm and provided as much information as she could. But, upon reflection, what she learned was that collaborating with the principal, and at the very least keeping her in the loop, would have streamlined the process and avoided the awkward situation for the principal of not knowing what was going on during a crisis situation in the school. The assistant principal also realized that because the principal had dealt with many emergency situations over the years, she had a wealth of knowledge that would have been helpful. Because this assistant principal was open and reflective, and the principal was not about to assign blame when the important thing was that the situation had run smoothly, the assistant principal continued to grow as an administrator and was highly effective in dealing with other emergency situations.

No One Crisis is the Same as the Next

Crisis and emergency situations come in many different ways and always when least expected. Weather-related emergency situations often cannot be anticipated but can have devastating consequences if not handled properly. Assistant principals need to be well versed on emergency preparedness procedures for all situations, including tornados, power outages, blizzards, and flooding. Schools that are overcapacity and have portable classrooms need emergency plans that deal with this complication as a lockdown situation may work differently in a trailer or portable classroom. In some situations, evacuating to a gym area can be the safest place to be; in other situations, it may be the most dangerous area in a school, depending on the specifics of the emergency.

Assistant principals need to be able to think of everything, including the safety of students outdoors in physical education classes, portable classrooms or anyone in the building with special needs in the event of an evacuation. Students or staff in wheelchairs or with limited mobility need individuals specifically designated to ensure they are evacuated safely in emergencies. Each school needs to have a comprehensive emergency plan and it is critical that in addition to being very familiar with protocols and procedures, each assistant principal does some "what if" thinking.

As medical emergencies are becoming increasingly frequent in schools, plans and protocols need to be established to deal with these issues. Although an asthma attack can seem like a mild inconvenience in some cases, it can also be life-threatening and always need to be taken seriously. Allergic reactions, broken bones, head injuries, and other complications almost seem like routine occurrences in schools on a daily basis, but how they are handled can speak volumes. Having an efficient system in place and protocols for calling for help can be lifesaving measures in a school. In many schools, defibrillators are being installed and training is critical. It is also essential that assistant principals know who in their building is certified in cardiopulmonary resuscitation (CPR), as well medical emergency management.

In one school, a quick-thinking assistant principal and school nurse identified that a female staff member was having a heart attack, despite the fact that she was extremely fit, had atypical symptoms, and no preexisting conditions that would indicate heart issues. A call was made to 911 immediately. The assistant principal happened to have aspirin in his desk (actually given to him by a colleague as a joke) and the nurse had the teacher take it. The insightful intuition of the assistant principal and nurse, quick medical attention, and aspirin may have saved her life.

It is important for schools to have procedures in place to keep students out of the hallways in the event of any situation or medical emergency where privacy or lack of intrusion is critical. Being able to think quickly and get appropriate support is essential. In most cases, an in-school healthcare provider is the best person to determine when 911 needs to be called, but it is always better to err on the side of caution when health and safety are in question, as hesitating a few minutes could potentially turn something into a life-threatening situation.

Every assistant principal needs to be keenly aware that at any time he or she may be called upon to make important decisions in an emergency situation. Although crisis training and effective leadership skills are essential, in a true emergency the assistant principal's core values and ability to remain calm regardless of the situation may determine how the crisis is handled.

14

Creating Opportunities: Is There a Road Map Out There?

The career journey should not be random—it should come with a plan where you recognize the opportunity landmarks.

Wanted: A Career GPS

An administrator's ongoing professional development is often dependent upon the opportunities that are available to the administrator, whether the administrator creates her own opportunities or has the guidance of others along the way. Sometimes an assistant principal is fortunate enough to have a mentor who actually maps out a career plan for him, often beginning long before they actually become an assistant principal. This kind of road map can be an actual timeline of courses, trainings, and opportunities to pursue, and can eventually turn into a viable resume. The mentor can be a trusted advisor who helps guide the assistant principal and can serve as a nonevaluative, nonjudgmental support throughout the assistant principal's career.

Unfortunately, most assistant principals don't have this intense level of guidance. Most assistant principals figure out on their own their best course for pursuing experiences and opportunities to keep them learning, engaged, and open to other possibilities. Which experiences, trainings, presentations, and networking opportunities make the most sense for the assistant principal for their optimal professional development? And how does the assistant principal recognize the right choices in the various stages of their career? The road map is rarely obvious.

The Principal as Tour Guide

An open, honest, and ongoing dialog with the principal continues to be one of the best resources and supports an assistant principal can have, providing they have a principal who is invested in professional growth, development, and opportunities for the assistant principal. This can be an encouraging and honest exchange and relationship or a highly frustrating one, depending on how it plays out over time. The assistant principal and principal may have very different perspectives on where the assistant principal is in their professional development and what their career trajectory should and could be. The assistant principal wants to be able to control his professional destiny. But he should not lose sight of the fact that the principal was once in his position and has already climbed this rung of the professional ladder as well as observed others who have also done this. It doesn't always make the principal the expert, but does it makes them the beneficiary of a range of experiences. Effective, secure principals are as willing to share the mistakes they made in career advancement as they are their successes. This is a time when both parties need to be good listeners and really understand each other's perspective.

In the worst-case scenario, the principal does not see the assistant principal as possessing the abilities, talents, and strengths to progress beyond her current position, which can be counterproductive for the ambitious assistant principal. Or, it can be a reality check for the assistant principal who erroneously thinks she knows it all and is prepared to move on to a principalship or another position of advancement. The truth is she may have huge gaps in her experiences and skill set. If the communication between the parties isn't straightforward and candid, neither party benefits. But this potential disconnect can be a test of the principal–assistant principal relationship. It is never easy for anyone to hear that they lack fundamental skills, traits, or experiences to advance in their career. Likewise, although a principal owes their mentee honesty, it is sometimes challenging to find a constructive way to explain major skill gaps.

One particular assistant principal saw herself as potential principal material. She was a creative problem solver, and worked tirelessly as an advocate for her students. She was affable, organized, and willing to take on new challenges. Yet she had not taught in a discipline associated with academic rigor, and as an administrator, had not really augmented her understanding of specific content areas. Although this assistant principal considered herself an instructional leader, she had not served as a department chair, and lacked a nuanced understanding of instructional practices. The principal recognized this deficit and approached the subject with the assistant principal respectfully but honestly. He communicated that that the assistant principal was not going to garner the full respect of the staff until she made this a primary focus of her responsibilities and professional development. He suggested that she work on a specific project related to a new math curriculum and lead the rollout and data analysis with the content team. Although difficult to accept, this frank conversation became a turning point in the career of the assistant principal. Aligning what the assistant principal wanted with how the principal saw it was critical in the assistant principal's professional development and potential advancement opportunities.

Opportunity Comes in Different Packages for Different Reasons

Having long-range plans and goals is always a productive and positive thing to do for anyone, but particularly for the assistant principal with career aspirations needing professional guidance and direction. This is not necessarily about looking toward the next assignment or rung on the administrative ladder, but about demonstrating excellence in all aspects of the current job. A realistic and reasonable goal may be a career path and destination as an assistant principal, an option explored in greater detail in Chapter 15. In this instance, creating opportunities is about the assistant principal taking on roles, projects, and tasks that round out the assistant principal's leadership experiences, or address the chinks in her personal administrative armor. It is not truly an "opportunity" if it is in an administrative area in which the assistant principal is already skilled, it's only more experience.

Early in his administrative career, an assistant principal had an opportunity he sensed would not only serve the school, but represented an interesting challenge. He was approached by his principal to write an extensive application for a large federal grant. Although he was generally an effective writer, he had never authored this sort of technical document and coordinated all of the requisite data that came with it. Although it was an add-on to his current duties, he also recognized that it would allow him to coordinate a large group of stakeholders, have the chance to work with respected central office administrators, and add to his administrative resume. Even though it required a tremendous amount of time and effort over a 2-month period, it afforded him a unique look at the "big picture" of school leadership. Even better, the leadership opportunity continued when the application was successful, and he became the administrative point person of a significant process change within the school.

Sometimes highly effective and competent assistant principals are unknown to others outside of their school. Principals can be of assistance when they delegate attendance at a meeting to the assistant principal, or better yet ask the assistant principal to accompany him and then discuss and process the experience. Regardless of whether the assistant principal is representing the school or attending a district-level meeting as an observer, it can be a learning experience and a networking opportunity. Principals who actively promote their assistant principals accomplishments are cognizant of the need to introduce their assistant principals to the higher-ups in the district. This exposure can give the assistant principal the opportunity to become a known entity, which can make a big difference if he seeks a different position in the district. It is extremely important for the principal to let superiors know when the assistant principal is doing a great job and where he sees the assistant principal's potential.

One principal told his assistant principal that when he himself was an assistant principal, he would get very frustrated when his principal repeatedly took credit for his ideas and innovative practices. He felt that he worked very hard for the school, but was never acknowledged, either privately or publicly, for his many contributions. When this assistant principal became a principal, he made it a common practice to always give the assistant principals who worked with him credit for programs, accomplishments, and handling of specific situations. His assistant principals really valued these accolades, particularly because this was not a principal known for giving "atta-boys." But his modeling of this very positive behavior, like ripples in a pond, were continued by the assistant principals he mentored as they gave teachers credit for their ideas and accomplishments. They also made sure to let teachers know when the principal positively commented to others about them. Those of the assistant principals he mentored who went on to become principals modeled this same practice in their own schools. Perhaps what the assistant principals valued so much about this principal was that when things didn't go well, he never publicly blamed the assistant principal but rather took responsibility for what went wrong and then worked with the assistant principal privately to solve the issue and make sure it wasn't repeated. This was a case where everyone benefited.

Asking for Directions Before You Get Lost

It is important for assistant principals to understand the professional resources that exist within their local system, as well as that are available from national administrative or curriculum organizations. These can be the resources that provide the missing pieces in the development of the assistant principal as an educational and instructional leader. These training opportunities may mean the difference between being prepared as a leader or stagnating and not moving forward in professional development. Much of the responsibility to pursue outside resources falls on the assistant principal, but the principal can provide valuable support in this area as they generally are more acquainted with professional organizations and opportunities that are available. In addition, a suggestion or nudge from the principal about a professional development opportunity can motivate the more reluctant assistant principal to try something new and the highly motivated assistant principal is usually eager for the support and recommendation.

In addition to the resources that they provide, becoming actively engaged in a professional organization can open doors for assistant principals. Although some administrators do not view what they do as unique, others take the risk to put themselves out there and present at conferences on an effective strategy, a new way of approaching an old problem, or a best practice in a specific area. As one assistant principal characterized it, "My presentations are not rocket science, but I never cease to be amazed at the application it has for different people in situations different than my own." The risk taking and additional effort that is required in putting together a presentation is usually returned manyfold in the connections, networking, and sharing that invariably happens in these settings.

Assistant principals can usually find many of their most valuable resources online. It doesn't take much research to discover professional online blogs, networks, web pages, webcasts, twitters, and however the next generation of technology evolves as a means of connecting people with common interests and goals. These are resources that can be particularly important for the lone assistant principal in a school or assistant principals who work in small districts and may feel isolated and without a collegial network. This type of resource can provide a safe means to discuss, explore, and develop professional relationships and healthy discussions around topics of interest to assistant principals in a neutral, nonjudgmental forum.

Online communication can also be a highly productive way to gather input from peers and look for best practices that may be very different from what the assistant principal has experienced. Sometimes a simple question such as, "How do you deal with distributing lockers when there is not one for every child in the school?," can yield myriad creative ideas that help the assistant principal come up with a more creative solution to a seemingly mundane problem. In this case, one of the more creative solutions was "family lockers," where the youngest sibling in a school was issued a locker and siblings (but no more than two to a locker) shared. This seemingly simple solution eliminated issues of theft from lockers and actually became a family convenience when one sibling was absent and needed their books brought home. The assistant principal may never have come up with this solution alone, but a new network of colleagues proved to be a valuable asset and support.

Creating opportunities in administrative leadership is less about luck and chance, and more about planning, design, and persistence. It may begin with the assistant principal thoughtfully redefining what they view as an opportunity. But the relationship the assistant principal has with his principal may be at the core of his development and potential advancement. Assistant principals who work in supportive environments, or who have mentors actively involved in their development, may see that finding their professional road map is a relatively easy task. But for the assistant principal without guidance, seeking the right resources can be a critically important and sometimes daunting task. Ultimately, the benefits and opportunities can be extremely fulfilling and rewarding in their current position and what potentially follows in their career.

15

What Do I Want to Be When I Grow Up? Suppose It's an Assistant Principal?

The choice to be a career assistant principal is a valid one, but with this choice comes other important decisions.

I'm "Just" An Assistant Principal

Once an assistant principal gains some time and experience in the position, one of the inevitable questions is, "Where do I go from here?" As with most career choices, there are rarely easy answers and plenty of questions that come into play before a path is obvious. There are a number of considerations deciding to remain an assistant principal, and ways to successfully navigate this as an option and not a default position.

One ongoing, but primary issue surrounding "just being an assistant principal" is the mindset. Just ask any longtime assistant principal—the job is time-consuming, requires a variety of professional skills, and can be very rewarding. But many assistant principals feel the need to fight the perception that if they are not looking to be a principal, they are "settling" and are not passionate, committed, or ambitious enough. "I love what I do, but I always have this fear of being seen as Ed Rooney," quipped one assistant principal, referencing the stereotypical assistant principal in the film *Ferris Bueller's Day Off*. "How could being 'assistant' anything really be the pinnacle of a career?"

Another common misperception is that veteran assistant principals are strictly those individuals who didn't quite have the "stuff" to be a principal. Most educators understand that just isn't true. The main consideration for the assistant principal is putting aside the effects of these perceptions. Instead, if one chooses to be a career assistant principal or in a position other than principal, the decision should based on judgment grounded in one's reality and personal needs.

Why Have I Remained an Assistant Principal? Plenty of Good Reasons!

The most common reason assistant principals choose to remain in the position is the recognition that they cannot commit to the additional time that is required to be a successful principal. Many assistant principals are simply not willing to make this choice because it would be at the expense of family commitments or outside interests. One cannot put more time into the day. It is a smart administrator who realizes that adding additional responsibilities and time (and, at times stress and anxiety) come at the expense of something else.

One assistant principal who would be an excellent principal candidate understood this all too well. He had six children of his own, each with numerous interests and activities. He enjoyed his job as an assistant principal and realized very quickly that his focus could only be in so many places at once. He needed to leave each day by a certain time to uphold his end of the parental taxi service and to be involved in his children's activities. His principal understood and respected his commitment to his family, but this commitment did not keep him from being highly effective in his job. This assistant principal made a conscience choice to not pursue a principalship. This did not represent a sacrifice for him, as it struck a positive balance for him and his family.

An equally valid point of view is that of the assistant principal who finds passion in his work, but also has passions that constitute having "a life." One assistant principal had considered the principalship but was moving into the "empty nest" phase of her life. She and her husband enjoyed traveling, and despite the fact she was perceived as a strong principal candidate, she was comfortable with the status quo. She recognized that being a principal probably would not allow her the same luxury to travel around the country, and one day visit grandchildren for extended periods of time. She was perceived as a committed assistant principal who loved her connection to students and their families, but who also liked exercising four days a week and wanted time for local political involvement. "I respect people who make the choice to be principal, but I know it doesn't fit where I am." This conscientious weighing of priorities led her to a secure choice.

Another logical reason to remain in the assistant principal position versus seeking the principalship relates to the nature of the two jobs. Assistant principals tend to implement programs or are process oriented. They focus on task management and work more closely with fine details and day-to-day student issues. In contrast, principals tend to focus on the overall vision of the school, political and district-level issues, the school physical plant, and financial aspects. They also serve as the chief liaison to the parent community.

As a result, some assistant principals come to realize that their skill set better matches the work of the assistant principalship. Others don't want to give up the daily reward that comes with helping students successfully navigate the ins and outs of school or with working with parents. Some assistant principals don't want to deal with the trickier political landscape that comes with being a principal—parent groups, business organizations, the superintendent, and school board. In short, it's not a question of a willingness to devote the time and effort required to be principal. Some assistant principals simply have an "aha" moment where they come to realize that they actually like their job better than what they perceive the principal's job to be.

I'm a Career Assistant Principal—Am I Stuck?

Whatever the reason, when an administrator makes the decision to be a career assistant principal, there are things that can help the administrator make the most from this choice and avoid potential pitfalls. How do assistant principals keep their daily routines fresh and their minds open to new challenges? The basic answer begins with staying sharp on the ever-changing educational trends and practices. In his book *The Seven Habits of Highly Effective People*, Steven Covey describes this process as "sharpening the saw"—keeping your skill set fresh and adapting to new methodology. In the current education landscape, this means practicing data-driven decision making—not simply knowing how to operate the data program, but understanding the philosophy that goes along with process. It means keeping abreast of changing district, state, and federal mandates. It involves developing strategies for evolving high-stakes testing processes. Assistant principals, like most educators, are asked to attend training in all of these areas and more. The true test for a veteran assistant principal is whether he takes this new knowledge and becomes a practitioner of what he has learned, or does he allow the training manual to sit on the shelf.

Sometimes it's simply a matter of making the conscious decision that "I'm going to do something differently." One particular assistant principal had been an arts program coordinator, had a personal passion for the arts, and in his five years as an assistant principal had always supervised the fine arts department. He knew the teacher players and the nuances of the department; he could predict the conflicts and knew how to respond. When the time came in the summer for the principal and assistant principals to determine supervisory assignments, everyone assumed he would want to again take the arts department. The not-so-obvious choice was the opportunity to supervise science, a department with new leadership and interpersonal challenges. He didn't feel as comfortable with the science curriculum, but he saw an opportunity to mentor a new leader and work with a group of teachers that lacked cohesion. When several of the arts teachers pleaded with him to not give up their department, he was flattered but knew it was equally as beneficial to give them a fresh leadership perspective with another assistant principal. Change for change sake isn't always effective and change with opportunity for growth is high risk, but potentially offers high rewards.

Identifying new challenges as a career assistant principal may depend on guidance or sometimes the kick in the pants an assistant principal receives from her mentor principal. If the principal is a veteran leader and secure in her place in the community, there are numerous opportunities to give the assistant principal the "reins." Some principals designate an acting principal when they leave the building for at least a day, allowing the assistant principal to make higher-level decisions for a short period of time. Conversely, principals will often petition to have their capable career assistant principals serve as their designees in a district meeting or on a central office committee that usually is reserved for principals.

Working with the Principal and (Sometimes) as the Principal

The mentor principal can encourage the assistant principal to present at staff meetings, parent informational forums, and to the business community. Assistant principals with knowledge of the principal's overall personnel goals can play a significant role in the staffing allocation and hiring process. Many principals welcome the opportunity to delegate important "principal-like" responsibilities, but the main thing is an inherently trusting relationship between the two parties. And while a veteran assistant principal may take on important responsibilities not normally associated with being an assistant, with great power comes much responsibility. An assistant principal may be in charge for a day, or tasked with instruction leadership, but in the end the buck stops with the principal. A guiding question even the most capable assistant principal should consider in decisions big and small is "can my principal live with the results, regardless of what they are."

A different approach must be considered when the veteran career assistant principal finds herself paired with a novice principal or principal new to the school. In this situation, the veteran assistant principal is cast as the keeper of the school's institutional memory. The principal may be very dependent on the assistant principal at first, to navigate relationships with staff and the community, as well as to help him understand "how we have done things." But again, this can be a great growth experience for the assistant principal, or it can be a real disaster. In the midst of this very dilemma, one assistant principal came to this conclusion: "I find myself every day as the veteran having to consider three or more options. I can be the sage who gently reminded the principal the reasons behind why we've 'always done it that way,' I can be open-minded and consider a new option the principal is presenting, or I can be a roadblock and a 'defender of the status quo.'" There was a real challenge in this situation, because the veteran assistant principal had been part of the school community for many years and had been intricately involved in establishing the status quo of the school. But she also recognized that this new principal had been chosen for sound reasons, had been an effective change agent in his previous school, and, most importantly, had the title "principal" above his office door. The veteran assistant principal began to strike a nice balance between being the institutional memory of the school and being energized by new directions that she could help lead.

Another deliberate choice that can take a veteran assistant principal into new territory involves giving away their assignment. One assistant principal had been the master scheduler of the school for many years. There was great authority and responsibility associated with this role, but it was one that had grown routine and stale. She also recognized that one of her assistant principal colleagues had a talent for the organization required for this job. She approached the principal and suggested that the other assistant principal be given the chance to tackle the job. The veteran assistant principal offered to mentor the new scheduler assistant principal, and work side by side with him to be successful. She characterized it this way: "I was still working on the master schedule, which I enjoy, but I was also teaching, something I enjoy more." In some respects, she was taking a step in the direction of the principalship by mentoring her colleague, serving as the "go-to person" in a new way.

Making Difficult But Important Decisions

There are often situations where becoming a principal isn't a realistic career goal. In small districts where there are only one or two high schools, the competition may be so great that it's not even a consideration. In other districts, an interested assistant principal may never even be given the opportunity to interview based on politics or other mitigating factors. Some assistant principals who want to be a principal, find they need to apply to other districts or uproot and move before this career goal can be accomplished. The ideal situation is when the assistant principal makes a choice to be an assistant principal, and it is not their default position.

In the final analysis, if an assistant principal chooses the career assistant principal route, the most important step associated with this choice is just that—to make it a conscious choice and make related decisions that maximize the benefits. Working with the mentor principal to defined and redefine the role, taking the risk that new opportunities present, and using veteran status judiciously can all combine to keeping the job fresh and rewarding.

16

What Do I Want to Be When I Grow Up? Suppose It's a Principal?

Prospective principals don't wait for "fate to take them by the hand." They take the steps necessary to make their goal less about luck and more about design.

"When You Get to the Fork in the Road, Take It"

Many people become administrators with a clear focus that becoming a principal is their career goal. For others, it may be a vague interest or a timing and situational issue. Assistant principals with young families may choose to pace themselves and not seek opportunities, whereas others may be very comfortable in the assistant principal role and not want to be a principal (or just not yet). Regardless of the surrounding circumstances it is incumbent upon the principal to ensure that the assistant principal has every possible opportunity to be prepared and ready for a principalship when and if the opportunity presents itself.

For assistant principals who clearly desire to become principals, there may be a set of challenges that they have not thoroughly thought through. District norms play a huge part in what opportunities are available and assistant principals need to think about whether they will work within the constraints of where they currently work or look elsewhere. Large school systems generally have more opportunities for advancement than small districts. In many situations, being in the right place at the right time is the most significant factor in determining who becomes a principal. But in all cases, being prepared when opportunities present themselves is a must.

Sometimes administrators find themselves on a career path that takes them to places they never intended. One highly effective assistant principal was determined that she had no desire to be a principal and was looking for an easier commute closer to home and a change of venue as an assistant principal. She felt the physical demands and distance from where she lived to where she worked was wearing on her and she even considered going back to the classroom. An opportunity opened up to be an assistant principal in the school in her neighborhood that her own children had attended and this lateral move greatly appealed to her. She enjoyed 2 years at that school and was very popular among the staff and community as she had a clear understanding of the culture of the school. At the end of 2 years, the principal was offered a promotional opportunity and left the school. Although the assistant principal originally didn't think she wanted to be a principal, being a principal at this particular school was an opportunity she did not want to pass up and so she took a risk and threw her hat into the ring and applied for the position. The relationships she established served her well and she was selected principal of the school and is enjoying a successful tenure. Even though she didn't anticipate she would end up as a principal, her previous experiences had prepared her and when the right opportunity presented itself, she was ready for the challenge.

Being in the Right Place...

The path to the principalship is not always a clear one. In some districts, the norm is for an assistant principal at either a middle school or high school to become a middle school principal first to demonstrate mastery in that environment before moving on to a high school principalship. In many school systems, this is a valid model as it gives the new principal experience on a slightly smaller scale before tackling the myriad of issues in a complex high school environment. In other districts, this may be seen as a disconnect as it puts the rising principal out of the loop of high school policies, norms, and politics while they are at the middle school. This may also have the undesirable effect of pigeon-holing the assistant principal as a middle school administrator, and not allow potential movement to be a high school administrator at a future time. For these reasons, some assistant principals will wait until their best fit in a principalship materializes, rather than take the first opportunity that comes along.

In many districts, a sitting high school assistant principal is considered the best candidate for a high school principalship. This can be a smooth transition or backfire terribly. It often depends on the training, preparation, and capacity of the new principal and his ability to understand the differences between his old role and his new one. It can be very problematic when an assistant principal is promoted in the same school, as there may be jealousy or credibility issues. In this situation, many people will support the elevation of the assistant principal because they (sometimes erroneously) believe that they will maintain the status quo—he's the "devil they know." But when the familiar assistant principal begins to make changes based on his own vision or the direction in which he wants to lead the school, there can be disillusionment or resentment. The opposite end of the spectrum may also present a challenge. When an assistant principal is promoted to principal from another school or district it can result in a struggle with the cultural norms of the school. The possibilities are seemingly endless. Whatever way it plays out, it is a challenging transition.

One assistant principal was determined to be a principal and was going to do whatever it took. He had only taught for three years before he became an assistant principal and while he had many strong skills, he did not always have a realistic view of his own abilities or understand where he had some gaps. After his third year as an assistant principal he changed schools to get a different experience. In his impatience, he began applying for principal-ships as they opened, even if the schools were not a good match with his experiences. After two unsuccessful interviews he got frustrated, applied to another district, and accepted the principalship of an extremely challenging inner city high school. He worked in that district for two years, and although he struggled, he grew a great deal professionally and gained a better per-spective on his abilities and the challenges of the job of the principal. He was rehired in the district he had worked in originally at a challenging high school and has been extremely successful. Although the route he took was not one he anticipated having to take, it ended up being a very positive move for him and it gave him a more global perspective.

...At the Right Time

For many assistant principals, timing is everything. Assistant principals need to think carefully about what is going on in their lives if they are con-sidering applying for a principalship. There is never a perfect time, but for assistant principals with young families, making sure all supports are in place for their family is a huge consideration. For an assistant principal purs-ing a PhD, that often tedious and time-consuming endeavor may supersede any ambitions to be a principal in the interests of time and sanity. Although the evening demands of an assistant principal may be considerable between meetings, chaperoning athletics, and other events, they pale in comparison to the schedule of a principal. Every new principal is going to need physical and emotional support from the people closest to them outside of the school building and for people with families, it truly needs to be a family decision. A supportive spouse or significant other can make all the difference in the effectiveness of a principal.

One very successful principal, who enjoyed a very long tenure, acknowl-edged that he knew more about the students in his school when his children were growing up, than he did about his own kids and it was one of his great-est regrets. Another principal passed up several opportunities to be a prin-cipal until she felt her children were old enough and appropriate supports were in place for it to work for her family. Her husband traveled in his job and she realized pursuing a principalship would not be fair to her family un-til her children were older. Once she became a principal, she always consult-ed with her children's schools before scheduling events like Back-to-School Night, awards programs, and other activities that could be major conflicts. When her son was in high school, she went as far as to let her community know that if she missed a football game, it was because it conflicted with her son's games and he had to come first to her. Although not all members of the school community understood, the majority recognized that she needed to put being a parent before being an educator. To be an effective principal for their children, she needed be an effective parent for her own.

The Prospective Principal (and Boy Scout) Motto: Be Prepared

Some assistant principals are fortunate enough to possess a unique skill set or previous experiences that make them a perfect fit for a particular principalship. A school may have an academy program that needs fine-tuning and there is an assistant principal with significant experiences in that specific area. Or a school might have a specialized magnet program and an assistant principal is certified and an expert in that particular subject matter, making that assistant principal a compelling candidate for that position. Having worked or grown up in a particular community also can help make a powerful connection as you are seen as "one of us" and someone who will understand the unique challenges of the community. In some cases, the race or ethnicity of a candidate, or their affinity for a particular language, may give them a leg up for a specific school. Clearly, a school with a large Latino population would benefit from having a principal who spoke Spanish, but this is neither the sole requirement nor a recipe for success. Principals are rarely hired for singular reasons. The overall match of the candidate's skills to the needs of the community is often the prime consideration.

The best possible preparation for the principalship is to be an outstanding assistant principal. Strong principals give assistant principals every opportunity to have a variety of experiences that allow them to demonstrate leadership. But assistant principals who wish to be considered for the principalship need to work with their principal mentors to make this goal a reality. Transparency about this desire is important and principals need to be prepared to be supportive, even if it means they will eventually lose an excellent assistant principal.

Having as many leadership and principal-type experiences prior to applying to be considered for a principalship helps to build a resume as well as a wealth of resources to deal with issues as they arise. Examples include facilitation of a key goal on the school's strategic improvement plan, representing the principal at important meetings or presenting data for a parent group. If the principal is on leave for an extended period of time, being designated as the acting principal gives the assistant principal a short but important glimpse into the world of the principal.

Assistant principals who want to be a principal, need to show initiative and not be afraid to take on new responsibilities or try new things. It is also important for the assistant principal to let his principal know of his aspirations so she can provide guidance and support. Assistant principals need to find a variety of ways to build their professional resume, so as to make them stronger candidates for the principalship. Many times there are district-level opportunities where an assistant principal can demonstrate leadership and have an opportunity to become better known around the district. These opportunities may be in the form of a committee or a task force, but should help the assistant principal build their personal repertoire of experiences. There also often are opportunities within state-level organizations to have varied experiences. In addition, professional development conferences are an outstanding way for the assistant principals to expand their knowledge base and to network with other professionals. Conferences and exploring the wide variety of professional growth opportunities available on a local, district, state, and national level are all viable ways for an assistant principal to continue to grow.

Like It or Not, Sometimes It's About Who You Know and How You Show

In medium and large school districts, networking with central office personnel who are key personnel decision makers becomes important. Oftentimes these school systems create central office workgroups and task-oriented teams that include school-based personnel. Rather than view these opportunities as chores that remove you from what you do in a school, treat them as an opportunity to understand the "big picture" of the larger political landscape, or demonstrate leadership skills to a wider audience as you never know who is watching. In one instance, an assistant principal who was a strong principal candidate thought her own principal was not advocating for her on a higher level. Rather than circumvent the norms of the promotion process by having conversations around her principal, she applied to serve on a central office data task force. As a result, the "powers that be" were given the opportunity to see her skill in presentational settings and a strong collaborative ability that they probably would not have seen or heard about otherwise.

There are very specific mechanics for the next step in this process, including creating a solid resume, writing an effective cover letter, and preparing for the interview process. There are many resources available for resume development and models of cover letters. Interviews can range from a chat with the superintendent or school board, to a highly competitive panel interview consisting of dozens of stakeholders, including parents, students, teachers, and community members associated with the school. Regardless of the structure of the interview process, the assistant principal needs to do her homework and understand what type of interview structure they will be entering into.

Equally as important is for the assistant principal to be up to speed and highly knowledgeable about the school and community where he is applying to be a principal. Investigating the school's student performance data and navigating their website can paint an important picture of the school climate and culture. Gathering as many resources as possible, talking to people who work in the school, and (if appropriate) the current leadership of the school allows the resourceful assistant principal to have a pretty good idea what will be asked in the interview.

One successful principal was asked many years later, by someone who was on the interview panel, if she had been given the specific questions ahead of time. The new principal was taken aback. She had done her homework so thoroughly that it was questioned if she had cheated on the interview, when in fact her research skills, previous experiences, and gut instincts made her a perfect fit for that particular principalship. She soon realized that this inquiry was actually the ultimate compliment on her preparation for the interview.

As with any interview, there may be unknown factors that influence the outcome and determine who gets a particular position. Many times this has little to do with the candidates and more to do with other circumstances, such as the preference of a particular board member, a bias by the superintendent, or something that may never come to light. It is not uncommon to have a highly qualified candidate who simply is not a good fit for that particular community. While this is challenging for the candidate to understand or accept, the reasoning can be sound. Regardless of the outcome, it is incumbent upon the assistant principal to be gracious even if unsuccessful. The assistant principal who wins the principalship needs to remember that now he actually has to do the job.

17

"I Love My Job, But..."

How to avoid making your job your life.

It's All About Time

Most people are drawn to education because they want to work with children. Teachers are individuals who have a passion for the subjects they teach; spend hours planning lessons and creating just the right experience to make the subject clear, engaging, interesting, and fun for students. But as is true of many professions, the harder you work, the more you're given to do. If you demonstrate competency as a teacher and become an administrator, the assumption is that you can handle even more responsibilities and greater challenges. In many cases this is absolutely correct, but at what cost personally?

One challenge of school administration is that the amount of time you could devote to working at and serving your school can be a bottomless well. There is always another project to complete, another event that you could be attending, another observation to write up, meetings to prepare for, data to analyze, and an infinite number of things that, given the time, you would love to get in front of. This is exacerbated by the fact that if an assistant principal aspires to the principalship, what they usually observe in their principal role model is a professional who has even more time commitments and constituents. Is balance between being a committed administrator and having a life possible? How can the principal guide the assistant principal in maintaining this delicate balance? Like most issues with no set answer, the challenge lies in how to structure that commitment while dedicating quality time to family, friends, exercise, hobbies, and outside pursuits.

In some districts, the first year as a new assistant principal is essentially a yearlong internship. Much of what happens is trial by fire and most experiences are new ones. The assistant principal is challenged to do everything for the very first time—be it developing a testing plan, a bell schedule, writing a crisis plan, dealing with irate parents, or working with student discipline. The multifaceted job of the assistant principal can be absolutely overwhelming and the time commitments can be exorbitant. In those districts where there is a probationary status for becoming an administrator, the challenge takes on an additional degree of difficulty. One assistant principal characterized it this way: "For those two years I was a probationary administrator, I felt like I had two jobs—my actual position as an administrator and a second part-time job learning about my position, attending required training, and preparing for my twelve probationary evaluation meetings." As a result, this same assistant principal maintains that, while the position of the assistant principal in his district doesn't get easier after the first two years, he thought the balance of time became more manageable.

It's Really All About How I Coordinate My Time with Others

Effective (and humane) principals recognize this and structure responsibilities in a way that doesn't overwhelm the new assistant principal or even veteran assistant principals as time goes on. Dumping everything on the new guy just doesn't work; no one can juggle all of the balls without dropping some from time to time. Likewise, piling every complex or high-stakes task on the most senior or accomplished assistant principal is not a recipe for success. Principals need to set clear but reasonable expectations for assignments, including attendance at school events beyond the school day. At regular intervals throughout the school year, they should also revisit the relative balance of assignments, and perhaps shift a few responsibilities from one assistant principal's plate to the plate of another.

One veteran assistant principal was guided by his principal to an "aha" moment about his administrative duties that really changed how he saw his role. As a rookie assistant principal he was assigned some of the more basic-level school operational tasks, such as the school master calendar and assigning chaperone duties. As the years went on, he had additional leadership responsibilities added to his plate, but continued to insist that he handle the other basic tasks. After all, he knew how to do it, and it was now relatively easy for him. What he didn't realize was that his new responsibilities were leaving him with less and less time to accomplish the other basic tasks. Although he certainly did these things well, all things being equal, all things were no longer equal. He wasn't giving himself permission to relinquish these duties to someone else. When his day had become unending and unmanageable, it took his principal to be quietly insistent. Yes, he did a great job with the bell schedule, but increasingly it was important for him to have additional time to focus on other tasks. More importantly, another novice assistant principal needed to have the same experience with basic tasks that he once had. And ironically, when he allowed himself to take things off his plate (a difficult task for many, to be sure), he actually found more meaning in the aspects of his job that he retained.

Administrative attendance at important school functions may be non-negotiable and people need to know far enough in advance so personal arrangements can be made. Certain events such as Back-to-School-Night, Homecoming, parent orientation, and graduation, are times when the entire administrative team probably needs to be present. Key athletic events, with the potential for issues with crowd control or anticipated problems based on school rivalries, are times when it may be reasonable to have increased coverage from assistant principals. But in general, when events are divided up, the principal will most certainly have a heavier load as the community almost always wants to see the principal at as many events as possible. Of course if the play is four nights and the principal attends the first night, the other three nights the parents will say, "Look at that! He doesn't even care enough to come see the play." Some things you just can't win.

When teams work together on event coverage, obviously everyone benefits. Much like the distribution of responsibilities, who covers which events needs to be a collaborative decision where all members of the administrative team gather together with schedules and personal calendars. The principal needs to be very specific, transparent, crystal clear, and above all reasonable about his expectations for attendance at school functions and events. This also needs to be discussed with enough lead time for assistant principals to be able to plan accordingly. All team members should have the opportunity to put their priorities and limitations out front so that fair and equitable decisions can be made. Members of the team have families and personal commitments, which need to be respected as much as possible.

One assistant principal let his administrative colleagues know that if he had to cover a Thursday evening event, he needed to have advance notice and hire a babysitter, as his wife had a standing commitment every Thursday night. Another assistant principal, with school-age children, needed to be able to schedule around his own children's events as much as possible. A third assistant principal lived an hour away, so she preferred coverage of after-school activities versus evening ones. She was also willing to do longer weekend activities versus coming back to school for multiple evenings during the week. Every team member has his or her own considerations, priorities, and personal plans to work around. But what this shouldn't mean is that the assistant principal who isn't married who happens to live close to the school gets extra duties because he doesn't have as many family commitments. Everyone needs to be respected and their personal time needs to be valued, with the understanding that the needs of the school must be met and the jobs must get done.

If one assistant principal is seen as not doing his fair share of school projects, assignments, or coverage, it is incumbent upon the principal to address this with him. If his professionalism is in question, it can become an evaluation issue and must be addressed immediately as it has the potential to erode or prevent effective team dynamics.

OK, So It's REALLY All About How and When I Structure My Day, in General

Some assistant principals believe that at the end of the day they should never leave school before the principal. Assistant principals, who are true professionals and go the extra mile, should not feel guilty leaving at the end of what is effectively their duty day. In many cases, people make choices about staying late. For assistant principals with young families, their preference may be to stay later to make sure they don't have to take work home with them. That way time at home is truly family time. For assistant principals with older or grown children, they may prefer to leave earlier and plan to do some work at home in the evening, perhaps while their own children are doing homework. Still other assistant principals like the early morning before their family awakes or other staff arrives for important, uninterrupted time to think and focus. As long as important work gets done in a timely manner, and the school day and events are appropriately covered, it should not matter what time people leave, within reason.

Spending more time at school does not always equate to doing a better job. Smart principals who work with assistant principals with a strong work ethic strongly encourage their assistant principals to go home at the end of the day, to make sure they do, indeed, have a life. Or better yet, they walk out with them. One assistant principal was under the assumption that his principal was pleased if he was still at his desk working every day as she walked out the door. He observed the other assistant principals around him who also worked long hours and assumed that this was the expectation, regardless of deadlines or work that was due. In fact, the principal grew concerned that this first-year assistant principal needed to keep his job in perspective so as to be more effective. She worried that the assistant principal was not spending enough time with his young family and had a long talk with him about how to prioritize more effectively. Assistant principals need to be reminded that the pile you leave on your desk in the evening can usually wait until the next day. It is virtually impossible for most people to actually leave an empty desk day after day.

One principal enjoyed coming into school on Sunday mornings and plowing through piles of work without distractions. He truly found this to be a productive time to reflect and get ready for the week ahead. This principal certainly did not expect his assistant principals to join him; in fact, if they did, it would have defeated his purpose for coming in.

The True Bigger Picture

As employee health and wellness becomes increasingly important, principals need to model good habits and encourage their assistant principals to do the same. One principal had a standing lunch appointment with his assistant principals after the student lunch periods were over, so as to discuss school issues and have some bonding and downtime. This practice also encouraged his administrative team to eat a reasonable lunch at a reasonable pace rather than eating junk food on the run or grazing on students' French fries in the cafeteria. Another principal managed to schedule gym time at the end of the day several times a week and encouraged his team to do the same. In another school a "Biggest Loser" challenge was posed to the faculty and the administrative team participated, to the delight of the staff.

Regardless of the healthy regimen or activity that brings balance to the administrator, many cite one critical component to ensure that it's successful—making the time. Many assistant principals discuss how a new school or calendar year brings the best of intentions as far as healthy habits are concerned. But the further along many administrators get, the more they allow their job responsibilities to edge out those life activities that wrongly become classified as "nice, but optional." One assistant principal admitted that it wasn't until he placed his every-other-day workout in his online schedule and instructed his secretary to protect that time at all costs (unless there was a crisis), that he truly made consistent time for himself. Another assistant principal who did the same thing quipped, "At first I felt guilty knowing there was work to be done. But what I soon realized is that I came home to my family energized, more positive, and just in a better frame of mind." Also, as a result of this, his wife minded less when he'd check his e-mail or look at paperwork later in the evening.

It can often be difficult for administrators to schedule important doctor, dental, or other personal appointments. There needs to be flexibility for the assistant principal to take care of these appointments without guilt, particularly those that are health-related. Effective and supportive teams cover events for each other and provide flexibility when needed. This works unless one or more assistant principals are seen as taking advantage and not pulling their weight.

All in the Family

For some assistant principals, bringing family to school events is a way to do their job and share some of the more enjoyable aspects of being an assistant principal with their family. One assistant principal frequently brought her two elementary-age children to school events. School staff found jobs for them and they enjoyed feeling important and a part of their mom's school life. One child became a ticket-taker at games, under the supervision of the staff member and she was paid five dollars a game for her help. The other child got to be a helper during basketball games and got a kick out of wearing a special T-shirt and bringing water to the players. This was win–win for the assistant principal as her children were of an age where they thought this was great fun and she didn't feel guilty leaving them on those evenings.

For school administrators, having a supportive spouse or significant other can make a huge difference, particularly at the times of the year when time demands are excessive. One assistant principal frequently was joined at school events by her husband. Their children were grown and he enjoyed attending athletic events and plays with her, although he passed on events that were of less interest to him and (obviously) evening meetings. His attendance spoke volumes not only about his support, but he became a regular fixture in the school, which increased her feeling of connectedness to her job. It also made covering outside events seem like less of a chore when her spouse attended with her.

One assistant principal recognized that as she moved from the classroom to the main office, the ebb and flow of her work life was about to change. Rather than allowing her husband and children just see this unfold or "get used to it," she took the time to have a family conference to explain the changes. She wouldn't be locking herself in the study any more with piles of essays to grade, and spending most Sunday evenings planning lessons for the week. But she would be going back to school one or two evenings a week for sports and other activities. She might not have the ability to drive her kids to all of their practices immediately after school, but she would have more flexibility in the day to attend their awards assemblies or take them to the orthodontist. More unanticipated works demands would pop up, but she would make their Tuesday evening family night activities a priority. In the end, she felt like the transition, while not perfect, was a little more predictable for her family.

Each assistant principal needs to set personal priorities and figure out how to do his job to the best of his abilities and still have energy left for family, a healthy lifestyle, and personal commitments. This isn't an easy thing to do but if it doesn't happen, the result is dissatisfaction, burnout, illness and sometimes far worse consequences. Long-term, when administrators don't maintain a balance in their life, they may find themselves with little to go home to or enjoy at the end of a productive career. At the end of the day, assistant principals and principals need to be able to distinguish between their jobs and their lives—it is not healthy when they are one and the same.

18

A Final Word

Some closing thoughts for both the assistant principal and principal.

Schools are complex organizations and effective school administrators must possess a unique skill set to successfully maneuver through them: intellect, passion, humor, intuition, patience, a sense of camaraderie, and the ability to inspire. Almost anyone can learn the craft of administration, but only the most excellent principals and assistant principals master the art of administration. And while the path to excellence is as unique as the individuals who pursue it, there are a few characteristics that are common.

So What's the Priority?

Each chapter of this book explored a different aspect of the development of assistant principals and the role that principals play. They all illustrated key points and made suggestions about "the most important factor" or "critical place to begin." If you're an assistant principal, at this point you may be wondering, "How can all of these things be the *most* important?" or perhaps "Of all these suggestions where do I truly begin?" One thought is that professional development should begin where it is most needed, namely with an assistant principal's most glaring deficiency or missing piece of skill set. Although the duties and responsibilities of the assistant principal should include opportunities where the assistant principal is most comfortable, real professional growth comes from the risk taking associated with new and unfamiliar projects. That is not to say that assistant principals should be thrown into the proverbial "deep end of the pool" with no life vest. But with a finite amount of time, energy, and attention to devote to their job, assistant principals may be best served by focusing on things that truly are new.

This, however, doesn't completely acknowledge reality. Schools are complicated places and are high-stakes environments. Students, parents, and staff all have towering expectations of their school leadership and there is very little margin for error. Assistant principals wish they had more time to take on proactive projects related to instructional leadership, but the reality is that the reactive day-to-day world usually takes precedent.

Educational leaders must be highly invested in making data-driven decisions. Many assistant principals recognize they must have a working knowledge of the nuts and bolts related to data management, but also need strategies on how to lead these efforts. To address this gap in their professional development, assistant principals may be inclined to attend a training seminar or conference. After the training, assistant principals triumphantly return to their school with the desire to "tinker" with their newfound knowledge and map out a plan for how to improve the school's instructional program.

Then reality sets in. Although the assistant principal was out of the building, a dozen student referrals came in that require followup. There are two parent conferences that were pushed back that must take place. There is a scheduled teacher observation and the daily rituals of lunch, hall, and bus duties, assorted meetings, and chaperoning the evening basketball game. What had been a proactive, long-term mindset and an opportunity for professional growth for the assistant principal eroded very quickly with the reactive day-to-day demands of the position. It would seem that the training and development of assistant principals is incompatible with the realities of their jobs. Are the two mutually exclusive?

Now More Than Ever: The Principal as Mentor

The answer, of course, is no. But merging these two seemingly competing priorities requires (dare we say it one final time?) principal mentors who see the benefit of professional development for their assistant principals. They actively work to run effective schools, but also don't miss opportunities to teach and mentor. The best principals view themselves as mentors, because the act of mentoring and teaching someone else always refines the skills of the one doing the mentoring and teaching. The best teachers learn the most from their students, and the principal–assistant principal relationship is no different.

The first priority of principals on any given day is to effectively lead and manage their school, not to figure out what situations present good learning opportunities for their assistant principals. No assistant principal ever went wrong keeping this question in mind: "What's the most effective way to improve teaching and learning for students?" The principal has the perspective to examine the big-picture needs of the school, and also provide growth opportunities for their assistant principals. Sometimes principals can gate-keep the assistant principals time, and work with the assistant principals to design one or two long-term, proactive, growth opportunities for the assistant principals to work on as time permits. They can help the assistant principals find the balance between the proactive and reactive aspects of their job. When principals embrace the mentor-trainer role, they are the individual that the assistant principals reflect with the most about their experiences.

Because the principal is part of the training and development equation doesn't guarantee the assistant principal's path will be a smooth one. A particularly difficult situation may occur when a brand new principal is mentoring a novice assistant principal. Although it can sometimes feel like the blind leading the blind, the resourceful principal sees this as an opportunity to move ahead in the direction of their vision with a (hopefully) willing copilot. The worst thing a new principal can do is assume he knows everything and not spend essential time listening to what is working in a school and then determining where a new course of action is needed. He needs to work to build the necessary buy-in from all constituent groups—staff, students, and parents—to be successful.

Creating an environment that encourages the professional development of assistant principals to be caring and innovative instructional leaders not only makes the job of the principal easier, but ultimately makes for a more well-run school, which benefits the entire school community. In the optimum situation, the assistant principal is eager to grow and learn and the principal is an enthusiastic teacher, creating the best possible professional environment, grounded in mutual respect, and with exciting and challenging growth opportunities. And when the principal moves on, he leaves highly skilled professionals prepared, trained, and ready to take on the leadership of the school.

The Ultimate Principal Responsibility: Mentor and Develop Your Replacement

Highly effective principals see mentoring their replacement as passing the administrative baton and as a crucial component of their role as principal. This awesome responsibility needs to be viewed as an integral part of the job, not an add-on, a necessary evil, or, worse yet, something outside of their job description that they can't be bothered with. The principal must, above all, be a teacher, a trainer, and a mentor to truly be a visionary and forward-thinking instructional leader. Conversely, the assistant principal must be open to professional growth opportunities and be willing and open to trying new things to stretch professionally. Depending on what trajectory the assistant principal sees their career taking, if the principalship is something they aspire to, they need to use every experience as a learning opportunity to grow and develop the specific skills needed to be a principal.

The secure and confident principal is always looking to the future and understands the benefits of ensuring that whenever they leave their current job and move on to something else, whether it is another position in or out of the district or even retirement, there is a highly competent and skilled leader ready and able to take on the stewardship of their school. This also comes with the knowledge that the principal will need to let go and that even the best school will experience some changes and adjustments under new leadership. A school needs to be viewed as a living, breathing organism, open and ready for renewal and changes that bring growth and, hopefully, improvement.

As long as a principal is fully prepared for the challenge, change can be a good thing. Even hiring one new staff member can change the school dynamics and the more new staff a new principal gets to hire, the more quickly it becomes "their" school. Sometimes a sitting principal needs to acknowledge that no matter how well she mentors her assistant principals, the district may have another idea of who should be her replacement when she leaves. In some cases, principals invest a great deal of time mentoring outstanding assistant principals only to lose them to principalships in other schools or districts. Although this makes the job of the principal more difficult, particularly if there is a revolving door of assistant principals, it is a tremendous tribute to their leadership and abilities as a mentor when their assistant principals move up to new positions and even become their peer as a principal.

Keeping It All in Perspective

Becoming an assistant principal can be a humbling experience. Most assistant principals were previously exceptional classroom teachers at the top of their game with positive relationships with students, parents, and their colleagues. They were secure in their position and found they often were the professional others turned to for advice. But the transition to administration can involve a steep learning curve, new challenges, and an unfamiliar daily routine. Sometimes the best perspective to have with this change of position is to simply embrace it and acknowledge that you have a lot to learn. Work to do the best you can each day, but cut yourself a break when things don't work out exactly as you envisioned. Be a good learner; spend more time listening and asking questions rather than expounding on what you already know and understand. Most good principals don't expect perfection in their new and even veteran assistant principals. Most understand all too well that everyone learns far more from their mistakes than from their successes. What good principals expect is that their assistant principals learn from their mistakes and don't make the same ones twice. Pride can sometimes get in the way of a good learning experience where humility opens the door.

Virtually every principal was once an assistant principal and it is extremely important that they never lose that perspective. The assistant principals job is challenging; it requires intelligence and patience. Days are usually full of excitement, occasional frustration, initiatives, roadblocks, exhaustion, and myriad other human experiences. Principals need to understand that although ultimately assistant principal decisions come back to the principal, assistant principals need to be supported and above all feel valued as both professionals and as human beings, with lives beyond the school day. The principal should act as a safety net for decisions an assistant principal makes, and because the ultimate responsibility doesn't rest with the assistant principal, give the assistant principal the latitude to grow, experiment, and learn from mistakes. Everyone's job in a school is easier when people communicate openly and effectively, are on the same page, put students first, and share a common vision for the future.

In the end, we hope this book has provided a variety of best practices that result in both the development of strong assistant principal leaders and strategies for effective principal mentors. The ultimate success of the education profession is dependent on the quality of those who work within its ranks, most specifically its leaders. In emphasizing the human and practical elements in an approach to mentoring, we realize that at the end of the day, after the students have gone home, the data is put away, the last phone call is made, and the last note is written, education is about forging productive relationships and building the capacity in all participants—our students, our staff, our parents, and, more specifically, our principal and assistant principal leadership.